FRANK LENTRICCHIA

ESSAYS ON HIS WORKS

WRITERS SERIES 33
SERIES EDITORS
JOSEPH PIVATO & ANTONIO D'ALFONSO

FRANK LENTRICCHIA

ESSAYS ON HIS WORKS

EDITED BY THOMAS DEPIETRO

GUERNICA

TORONTO — BUFFALO — LANCASTER (U.K.)

2011

Thomas DePietro, Guest editor
Guernica Editions Inc.
P.O. Box 117, Station P, Toronto (ON), Canada M5S 2S6
2250 Military Road, Tonawanda, N.Y. 14150-6000 U.S.A.

Distributors:
University of Toronto Press Distribution,
5201 Dufferin Street, Toronto (ON), Canada M3H 5T8
Gazelle Book Services, White Cross Mills, High Town,
Lancaster LA1 4XS U.K.

First edition.
Printed in Canada.

Legal Deposit –First Quarter
Library of Congress Catalog Card Number: 2010937398
Library and Archives Canada Cataloguing in Publication
Frank Lentricchia : esssays on his works / Thomas DePietro, editor.
(Writers series ; 33)
Includes bibliographical references.
ISBN 978-1-55071-312-1

1. Lentricchia, Frank—Criticism and interpretation.
I. DePietro, Thomas II. Series: Writers series (Toronto, Ont.) ; 33
PS3562.E4937Z55 2010   813'.54   C2010-906314-7

Contents

Acknowledgments

Philip Tinari's "Being Frank," from *Duke Magazine*, the university's alumni magazine, is published with the permission of the author. Kit Wallingford's "The Theater of the Self in *The Edge of Night*" appeared in slightly different form in the *American Quarterly*, and is reprinted with her permission. Vince Passaro's review of *Johnny Critelli* and *The Knifemen* originally appeared in *The New York Observer* and is reprinted with his permission. Fred L. Gardaphe's "Lentricchia's Gangsters" is adapted from his book, *From Wiseguys to Wise Men* (2006), and is printed with his permission. Thomas Hove's "Lentricchia's Melville Troubles" is a revised version of a review that appeared in *Melville Society Extracts*, and appears with the author's permission.

Introduction

When Frank Lentricchia edited a volume on Don DeLillo in 1991 and called it *Introducing Don DeLillo*, it struck long-time fans of DeLillo as a bit odd. We certainly needed no introduction to one of America's greatest novelists. After all, at the time, DeLillo had published almost ten novels, including such contemporary classics as *White Noise* (1985) and *Libra* (1988). Of course, the explanation for the title is obvious: Lentricchia wasn't introducing DeLillo to general readers. His volume addressed itself to the academy, where DeLillo had yet to receive the attention which he has since garnered in spades. So, the subtitle of this volume is intended in reverse. These essays introduce Lentricchia's work as a memoirist and novelist, not as a scholar and literary critic. Anyone who has spent time in literature departments in the last thirty years needs no introduction to Lentricchia's work in criticism and theory. But few in or out of the academy know Lentricchia's noncritical writing, which has been published in the last ten or so years mostly by small presses.

The articles included here vary in style and scope, and reflect the wide range of Lentricchia's thematic concerns as well as the breadth of critical approaches his work inspires. Philip Tinari's profile from the Duke University alumni magazine nicely sums up Frank the man, and neatly surveys his academic career, which is why it leads off the volume. It's all you need to know about Lentricchia's earlier work in relation to his subsequent pursuits. Tinari, like McAuliffe and DuBois, has a close relation to Lentricchia, having been one of his students at Duke. DuBois, who went on to do graduate work at Harvard, was also Lentricchia's student. And McAuliffe, most intimate of all, is literally married to her subject. All three pieces combine personal detail with critical insight, and DuBois and McAuliffe, in particular – whose essays were solicited for this volume – bring amazing verve and humor to their discussions of Lentricchia's fictional obsessions.

Early reviews reprinted here by Wallingford, Passaro, and Hove place Lentricchia's work in its literary-historical context. Wallingford notes the precedent for his confessions in the mid-century poets, such as Lowell and Berryman. Passaro locates Lentricchia among the masters of "self-loathing," from Poe to William Burroughs. And Hove meditates on Lentricchia's greatest agon, Herman Melville, whose life and work figure so brilliantly in *Lucchesi and The Whale*.

The longer articles in this book, most of

which are published for the first time, demonstrate the reach of Lentricchia's recurring concerns: ethnicity, identity, place, and the nature of the artistic process. The excerpt from Gardaphe's recent study of Italian-American gangsters in film and literature suggests that Lentricchia advances our understanding of this otherwise stereotyped figure in modern culture: Lentricchia's wiseguys transcend the popular type, and raise issues of sexuality and race not often found in such works. Birns also attends to Lentricchia's ethnic and social themes: how does Lentricchia's hometown of Utica signify in his novels? What's the importance of place to a writer clearly deracinated in so many ways?

Wellman and O'Hara/Masucci-MacKenzie focus on larger aesthetic ideas. Wellman pays attention to the importance of Don DeLillo's work to Lentricchia. They share a similar view of history, popular culture, and the relation of both to narrative structure and design. She also finds ample cause for placing Lentricchia in the grand tradition of Fitzgerald and others who seek to define the American experience. O'Hara and Masucci-MacKenzie, on the other hand, see in Lentricchia the eternal artistic struggle to define a self, articulated by great writers like Joyce, and pathologized by psychiatrists such as Lacan and Zizek. Melville, Fitzgerald, Lowell,

Joyce, DeLillo. Lentricchia's admirers aren't afraid to compare him to the greats. I hope the interview I conducted with Lentricchia covers some of the more mundane (but no less significant) ideas and issues inspired by his work. It's not often that an established and esteemed academic reinvents himself as Lentricchia has. His fictional voice is fresh and sharp, not at all dulled by the years of critical writing. Let this volume serve as both introduction and tribute.

Being Frank

PHILIP TINARI

Adorning the walls of his East Campus office are three paintings from the Duke art museum's permanent collection. One, a somber, disfigured nude in dark hues, was painted by a Duke art student in the late Sixties, shortly before his suicide. This is the favorite, the one he asked for; the other two were there already when he moved in 1993 from his earlier perch in the Allen Building. The room is adorned in mahogany, with a large desk, two walls of bookshelves, and a small, round table with chairs that barely reveal their institutional heritage. There is no computer, not even a typewriter – just yellow legal pads and a can of pencils. The office corner frames a poster advertising Ezra Pound's 1931 pamphlet "How to Read," with those three contentious words emblazoned on yellowing leaves in 40-point type. This is the office of Thomas Lucchesi, professor of American literature, writer of letters, visitor of moribund friends. A man who teaches college "only because [his] fiction is commercially untouchable," and who works tirelessly, if not productively, on some "experimental novel." A man who can deal more aptly with art than with life. A man whose passion to create can, time and again, isolate him and saddle him with anxiety. A self-fashioned "mad Ahab of reading," who searches desperately, in heartfelt scholarly prose, for the meaning within Melville's *Moby-Dick*. A man who sometimes sees his world through the prism of Ludwig Wittgenstein's *Philosophical Investigations*. But above all, a man whose love for life, for his intimates, and himself, endures.

In reality, it is the office of Frank Lentricchia A.M. 1963, Ph.D. 1966, Katherine Everett Gilbert Professor of literature, celebrated critic, novelist, master teacher, lover of high modernist poetry, and creator of Thomas Lucchesi. His work, especially a critical trilogy in the 1980s, has inspired many a fierce devotee of its own. In an angry testimonial published in 1996 he famously disavowed his status as a pre-eminent literary critic – and the entire notion of politically based, politically biased, politically correct scholarship, which he has been charged with inventing. Finally, he has turned to "close reading" and fiction writing as outlets for the literary passion he refused to let the academy contain. Lucchesi is the hero of Lentricchia's *Lucchesi and The Whale* (the "The," in reference to Melville's creation, takes its capital on purpose), published last year by Duke University Press. And for its author, Lucchesi "is an outgrowth of a preoccupation with the cost of shutting yourself down in order to practice total devotion to your work."

Lucchesi began with a few literary sketches culled from the author's dreams, and grew from there into a lyric fiction. Through it all, the awake Lentricchia was dealing with the baggage of a semester of Melville's *Moby-Dick*, during which "the book suddenly loomed before me as unteachable." Channeling frustration into inspiration, he says he began to think "this obsession with Melville would give some coherence to the various fragments of narrative that I had just put together. Inevitably, I came to the point where I realized that my character had to confront *Moby-Dick*, and that became the central drama of the book." He describes it finally as "the kind of narrative that sits on the border between realism and fantasy." An opera in four acts, the book opens with two sequences of dreams culled from the author's nightly travels, everything from a family of cannibalistic snakes to an evening at La Scala, where Lucchesi-the-writer is called to replace Pavarotti-the-singer. A comic interlude titled "Writer in Residence" separates these earlier forays from the following meat of the book, which is a critical reflection in the form of an obsessive monologue on Melville's *Moby-Dick*. In a few hundred words, Lucchesi is dismissed from his post at Central College at the behest of the dean and a certain "President Jan" who find his pedagogy, which consists of "repeated and strenuous exercise in deep aesthetic immersion," risible. "Chasing Melville," an animated spell of light-hearted criticism in Lucchesi's thinly disguised Lentricchian voice, takes up the central question of hyphenation. *Moby-Dick* is the totality, the aesthetic universe, in which Moby Dick, The Whale, resides. "It definitely stems from the terrible experience that I had with Melville in the classroom, not that any of it came out that well at the time," says Lentricchia. Lucchesi concludes with a meditation on "Sex and Wittgenstein," wherein the bookish professor woos an Alitalia flight attendant into midair lovemaking with his dazzling explications of philosophical nuance.

Lucchesi plays with the boundaries of book form, with the "structurality of the structure," to use some of the very parlance Lentricchia coined in his earlier incarnation as a literary theorist. To understand his playful irreverence toward established conventions and forms, one must go back a bit, to his revolutionary 1980s. Back then, when his mustache was full, Lentricchia used to anger and inspire in equal and vehement num-

14

bers. And to understand this polemical face of Frank Lentricchia, one must then go back even further, to his days at Duke as a graduate student under Professor Bernard Duffey.

In the old Duke English department, Lentricchia penned a historical master's thesis on the American reception of the poet Byron, which gave rise to his first published essay. A dissertation followed, and the book that sprung from it, *The Gaiety of Language: An Essay on the Radical Poetics of W.B. Yeats and Wallace Stevens*, was released only two years after he took his Ph.D. in 1966. Even in the book's title, traces of Lentricchia's double-edged obsession begin to shine. The pleasures of language and radicalism of artists and critics – the two strands that entwine his career – were present already in his first work of scholarship.

From his assistant professor's chairs at UCLA and then UC-Irvine, Lentricchia's early scholarship began to unfold. In *Robert Frost: Modern Poetics and the Landscapes of Self,* which he considers his "weakest book," he argued for Frost's place "as a welcome member in the company of Eliot, Stevens, and Yeats," as someone engaged with the literary and philosophical ideas of his day. Lentricchia waited nearly two years for the book to find a publisher; during this time he wrote *Robert Frost: A Bibliography, 1913-1974.*

Once the two works were published, in 1975 and 1976, Lentricchia says he grew bored. "It's sort of a motif in my life; I find myself written out in a certain vein and look for something else to do to keep myself interested." At Irvine, with the newly christened discipline of "critical theory" preparing to "stretch its mighty limbs and take over the stage of professional study on the literary side of the academy," Lentricchia didn't have to look far. "Theory" referred then to High Post-Structuralism, a wave of largely French thought that sought to debunk the fixity of text and the stability of language through its intricate formulae of Marxian, Freudian, and Nietzschean suspicion. Despite the strife it created, there was no single book to which a theory newcomer could turn for orientation, or in which a theory practitioner could see the historical landscape against which his work was being done.

No book, that is, until Lentricchia's *After the New Criticism* appeared in 1980. At once a roadmap for the uninitiated and a tome for the expert, it circulated as the Little Red Book of this particular cultural revolution. *After the New Criticism* tracks the development of the movement from Northrop Frye's *Anatomy of Criticism* through existentialism, phenomenology, and structuralism to post-structuralism. It concludes with chapters on Murray Krieger, E.D. Hirsch,

Paul DeMan, and Harold Bloom. It was the kind of book people bought to find out what was going on.

In providing an observer's account, Lentricchia also served up his own literary philosophy. "I ended up writing a polemical history, one which charged a number of practitioners of contemporary theory with idealism." Some of the book's harshest critiques, then, came not from the theory-averse, but from theory-lovers who were beginning to wonder whether their newly minted jargon could ever change the world.

Now famous in literary circles, Lentricchia moved to Rice University in 1982, and in another year had drafted an answer to his critics in *Criticism and Social Change*. The slim, 170-page book argues that literary scholars, as literary scholars, can and should contribute to the work of the left. "In the absence of a program or positive message in *After the New Criticism*," says Lentricchia, "it attempted to put something in place of what I didn't like." That "something" – the idea of humanist scholarship as a platform for "activist study, contentious study, study with a purpose in mind, ulterior political goals, study that would open up the canon, study that would recognize the multiplicity of American cultures, study on behalf of the denigrated and the downtrodden" – cleaved the academy in two.

Lentricchia and his insistence on blurring the line between scholarship and politics were excoriated by the Reagan-era cultural right. "I got some good strong corrosive footnotes from the wife of our current vice president, Lynne Cheney," director at the time of the National Endowment for the Humanities. In the years that followed, theory's second wave swelled, in which the textual irreverence of the now-hyphenless poststructuralism met the radical fervor of identity politics. If a single sentence couldn't have a fixed meaning outside language's "system of differences," how could anyone possibly dictate a list of great books? Bitter public debates broke out as Stanford University led the charge to revamp its Western Civ requirements, and schools across the country pondered the pertinence and fairness of the canon. "The whole story of political correctness in the university and the literary academy," Lentricchia notes, "was put at the door of this little blue book."

The book gave him renown as a figure of cultural discord. The jacket photograph bears his likeness in a tight-fitting golf shirt, arms crossed and biceps borne. Maureen Corrigan, in an early 1984 *Village Voice* review, coined the "Dirty Harry of contemporary literary theory" moniker that Lentricchia, eighteen years later, has not outlived. He remained suspicious of this media fixation – "it's as if one's personality were one's work!" – but such newfound academic celebrity wound up drawing him back to a Duke that was hovering on the brink of national prominence.

Lentricchia was lured back to his alma mater in 1984. It was a bold step for the university, the beginning of a commitment to a particular style of renegade scholarship that evokes both resentment and admiration from the wider community. He remembers his first public lecture as a Duke faculty member, over dinner at the nearby National Humanities Center. He outlined his thesis from *Criticism and Social Change*, and several of his new colleagues stomped angrily from the room.

As is sometimes forgotten, it was a suggestion from Lentricchia that brought Stanley Fish from Johns Hopkins to the department chairmanship he so notoriously inhabited between 1986 and 1991. Fish, who remained on the Duke faculty until accepting a deanship at the University of Illinois in Chicago in 1998, presided over what a 1992 external review committee called "a kind of engine or life-pump for the humanities at Duke, a supplier of intellectual energy and stimulation for the university at large." Hot hires proliferated, graduate applications increased fivefold, and the once sleepy Duke University

Press re-fashioned itself as a clearinghouse for cutting-edge scholarship. Lentricchia's other enduring recruitment suggestion was the appointment of Marxist critic Fredric Jameson to found and spearhead what grew into the Program in Literature, an interdisciplinary venture that incorporates comparative literature, literary theory, cultural studies, and film. More than fifteen years later, the program – into which Lentricchia himself transferred his appointment in 1993 – remains strong.

From his new digs at Duke, Lentricchia wrote the final piece of his critical trilogy, *Ariel and the Police*. With sections on Michel Foucault, William James, and Wallace Stevens, he says, "the book moved away from pure literary theory; it was a reading of Stevens' life and poetry in its cultural context." What shines through in *Ariel and the Police* is an obsession with the act of writing over and above its philosophical significance as expounded in *After the New Criticism* or its political value as defended in *Criticism and Social Change*. It represents less the end of Lentricchia the critic than the beginning of Lentricchia the writer. "That whole side of me came out then. I must have known that I was going to be bored soon, had done what I could do there, and was asking myself, okay, what next?" The following years saw the production of two edited volumes on Don DeLillo and *Critical Terms for Literary Study*, an undergraduate anthology that has proven his best-selling work. But the shadow of *Modernist Quartet* – a book on Frost, Stevens, Pound, and Eliot that had been under contract since 1982 – suddenly loomed before him as unwritable.

A set of personal and intellectual crises were afoot. Lentricchia faced mid-life anxieties as his marriage collapsed. He spent parts of the summer of 1991 at Mepkin Abbey, the Trappist monastery in South Carolina. He spent the fall semester of 1991 in New York teaching on a Duke-sponsored program for art students. All the while, he was writing a set of autobiographical meditations that would become his next book. "Literally," he recalls, "what started it was a commandment from a monk to write. I was leaving the monastery and he said, 'You have to tell the world about this, you have to write about it.' 'You're a writer,' he said. 'Write through this.' "

So Lentricchia undertook a project that departed significantly in scope and tenor from everything he had done in twenty years as a professor. "I felt myself launched into a totally different literary space, one in which I was writing about what actually happened. So it was not fiction in that sense, but I found myself writing about it in a way that released me from fact, so that I could explore my emotional reactions, so that I could explore what it meant for me to reflect upon myself at this stage. And I thought it was very seductive, I enjoyed it very much." He published one of these meditations in the journal *Raritan*, and presented another, to much chagrin and a quiet room, at Harvard's annual English Language Institute in 1993. "I think a number of people found it a breach of propriety, that level of personal revelation. That maybe you'd want to write this, but why the hell would you ever want to publish it? I think some people were, without telling me, embarrassed on my behalf that I should be doing this." The reflections were published in 1994 as *The Edge of Night: A Confession*. Lentricchia was more invigorated than apologetic. According to Clay Taliaferro, Duke dance professor and Lentricchia's friend, the catharsis set him free. "Frank lives the moment through and through, and this outburst was so necessary to his personal continuity. It was such a huge outburst, personally and publicly, and he never lost in the process any of his essence as a strong man full of love, full of spirit." Taliaferro is the only man to have played Lentricchia on stage, which he did in a 1994 dramatization of *The Edge of Night* by drama professor Jody McAuliffe. It was a time of literal as well as intellectual rebirth – Lentricchia and McAuliffe married, and their daughter, Maeve, was born in 1994.

A proleptic meditation on Foucault in the final essay of *Ariel and the Police* hints at the course Lentricchia's intellectual life would take in the wake of *The Edge of Night*: "Foucault's antidote is writing: not as a space for the preservation of identity and the assertion of voice, but as a labyrinth into which he can escape, to 'lose myself,' and, there, in the labyrinth never to have to be a self – write yourself off, as it were, 'write in order to have no face.' "

Within a few years, Lentricchia had turned his back on his status as critic and fashioned himself an advocate for, and creator of, art. He denied the criticism he had worked to create, and did so, ultimately, out of frustration with methods of criticism that hinged on moral superiority. The story goes that one day in the early 1990s, a graduate student opened class discussion in one of his seminars with the words, "The first thing we need to understand is that Faulkner was a racist." Vexed by what he considered narrow-minded reading, Lentricchia stopped teaching graduate students, and in the September/October 1996 issue of *Lingua Franca*, outlined his much-maligned objection to critical work as it was coming to be practiced: "The fun-

damental, if only implied, message of much literary criticism is self-righteous, and it takes this
form: 'T.S. Eliot is a homophobe and I am not.
Therefore, I am a better person than Eliot.
Imitate me, not Eliot.' To which the proper
response is: 'But T.S. Eliot could really write,
and you can't. Tell us truly, is there no filth in
your soul?'"

Lentricchia sought greener literary pastures
and, within four years, published three novels –
Johnny Critelli, *The Knifemen*, and *The Music of
the Inferno*. *Critelli*, which began as a sequel to
The Edge of Night tentatively titled *For My
Father*, was not far from Lentricchia's autobiographical fare. He remembers his thrill when
"after about two pages, I realized I was not writing a memoir, I was writing fiction, and that was
really exciting."

The Knifemen, inspired by the consuming
O.J. Simpson spectacle, was his attempt at
"something that was as far as possible from the
lyric mode of *Critelli*; something that was not
musical, but brutal, blunt as possible." The two
were published in the same volume by Scribner
in 1996, paving the way for Lentricchia's longest
sustained work of fiction, *The Music of the
Inferno*. In this "novel in the more traditional
sense," splashed against the historical canvas of
Utica, Lentricchia traces the story of Robert

Tagliaferro, a racially ambiguous orphan who lives alone in a bookstore.

After a decade of splashing his love for art in the face of critics run amok, Lentricchia is ready for a fusion of his several worlds. *Lucchesi and The Whale* hints at this: a work about a teacher and his students, one that combines literary criticism and a vague, curious kind of autobiography. Says Lentricchia of *Lucchesi*, "Maybe in this particular text I came back to a side of me that I had left behind when I started writing *The Edge of Night*, that I had run away from. Then I wanted to get as far away from literary criticism as possible. I wanted to do a kind of writing that would stem not from the rational, but from the fingertips or from the blood or from some other bodily fluid, but not from the brain, the rational brain. But maybe in *Lucchesi* I've married myself to myself."

One product of Lentricchia's pedagogic power is Andrew DuBois 1996, a Lentricchia student turned co-author, a humble Alabaman and Harvard Ph.D. candidate whose undergraduate and doctoral theses take up the "radical poetics" of John Ashbery and the high postmodernists (à la the young Lentricchia). "Frank's work is still activist," maintains DuBois, "in that it's always about art against whatever would try to squelch it out."

After re-writing *Modernist Quartet* as a volume for the *Cambridge History of American Literature*, DuBois is collaborating with Lentricchia once more, this time on an anthology, *Close Reading: The Reader*. It draws together landmark essays by formalists and deconstructionists alike. "The polemical point underneath it, without being explicit," argues Lentricchia, "is that the newer stuff, the newer modes of literary interpretation, are most persuasive when they do not break with the older formalist protocol, that there is not a great divide between contemporary schools of literary criticism and the older criticism." And as if this new contentiousness weren't enough, Lentricchia – together with McAuliffe – is hard at work on a critical book, *From Groundzeroland to Kleist: Studies in Transgressive Desire*. Centering on fiction and film, as well as real-life figures, the book will examine a definition of the artist as someone who acts, sometimes unwillingly, as a violator of the social order. "It is our contention that modernism grows steadily from early romantic preoccupations with the difference, the deviance, the uselessness of the artist – his break from all norms of his society: the artist, in other words, as seer whose ways of seeing and expression put him in sharp contrast to publicly held understanding and values." The project ties research to teaching, having inspired an eponymous course in the literature program, co-taught by Lentricchia and McAuliffe. "Bringing one's work to the undergraduate classroom is the greatest challenge of all," he says, "because it affords teachers the possibility of bringing what they're doing at the very edge of their minds to an audience which will test the clarity of their conception. And if you can do that with a good, strong undergraduate group, then you have succeeded in finding a style that makes your work available to literate people in general."

It's a statement that would be a long time coming from "mad Ahab" Thomas Lucchesi. But it's a sign that Frank Lentricchia has once again left one literary creation behind to build upon another.

The Theater of the Self
in *The Edge of Night*

KIT WALLINGFORD

In the now-famous dust jacket photograph of his *Criticism and Social Change*, a polo-shirted Frank Lentricchia stands, arms folded, staring just past the camera, the very picture of macho confrontationality. This self-mocking performance, a daring one for a literary critic in 1983, has been noted in forums as varied as the *New York Times Magazine* and *boundary 2*. Random House has packaged Lentricchia's *The Edge of Night*, which on the dust jacket is subtitled "A Confession," to take advantage of and to add to his notoriety. In addition to the soap opera title, the front flap quotes the *Times* (which was quoting the *Village Voice*) as naming him "the Dirty Harry of contemporary literary theory" – an appellation that has been as much savored and disdained as the photograph. The adulatory quotations on the back cover begin with "A street-smart literary strip-tease: St. Augustine meets *Raging Bull* via T.S. Eliot." The biographical note in the text lists some of his "controversial and acclaimed" books. And in the photograph for this book, he is wearing what appears to be a black T-shirt.

The book itself is hard to place generically. In *The Edge of Night*, Lentricchia plays with – performs, enacts – the dilemmas of subjectivity; indeed, one might say that the subject of the book, in addition to Frank Lentricchia, is subjectivity itself. And he links this troubled subject to the issue of presence and representation in writing. Who is the speaker of this book? *"L'ecriture, c'est moi,"* he writes, and the self-mocking tone acts neither to suggest a naive identification of author and speaker nor to condemn a reader's or writer's desire for such identification. And herein lies the merit of the book: knowing what he knows (which is formidable) Lentricchia acts out a character in search of a self he can live with. While he acts out this role, he reflects on it, and reflects on his reflecting on it, and theorizes the entire process. He dramatizes the fact that his self – and he defiantly uses that word "self" over and over again – does not exist apart from the reflecting or theorizing. Discussing his reply to a letter that apparently precipitated his writing the book, he says, "I don't tell him that I'd like to mix up the personal and the intellectual to the point where it would be impossible to separate them, not as an exercise in high-wire theory (this

I know how to do), but as an act of homage to the real state of my affairs." Here Lentricchia is problematizing the conflict between those who insist on the relevance of the personal in criticism and theory, and those who prefer their intellection in the form of abstraction.

He is also working out of the tradition of autobiography, and I find myself comparing his book not to previous writings of literary critics or even of Augustine, Rousseau, or Wordsworth, but rather to the so-called confessional poetry of Robert Lowell and his generation – especially that of the men. Reacting against what they considered the impersonality of the Pound-Eliot strain of high modernism, Lowell, Theodore Roethke, and John Berryman, among others, wrote poems that dealt unabashedly with personal experience. Some readers then, as now, reacted uncomfortably and disparagingly to the experience of encountering details of personal life in a place where they were accustomed to finding pleasantly arcane and allusive intellectual puzzles.

Like the confessional poets, Lentricchia embeds his self in the ground of family. Indeed, *The Edge of Night* begins much like Lowell's "91 Revere Street," the prose section of his landmark volume *Life Studies*. In both texts, the male protagonist first appears inside a home, surrounded by father and talkative mother, with grandparents and other relatives appearing through recollections. Family portraits are important; grandfathers are influential. Of course Lowell has a grand and famous family tradition against which to rebel, whereas Lentricchia wants to claim and celebrate his Italian-American working-class background. But both assume that family plays a role in the definition of self and that readers will welcome having the connections made available. Both understand the power of family members' words to structure identity, and neither hesitates to put words in relatives' mouths. Both struggle with and sometimes embrace the resulting self-awareness and its concomitant guilt. Both have things they need to confess.

Each writer assumes a personal – and perhaps general – value in making his confession public. But confessional writers run at least two risks: readers may find all confessional writing to be merely adolescent self-indulgence, or they may not like the "person" who appears in the text. The Lentricchia of *The Edge of Night* is hard to like, and he knows it; indeed, he depends on it. Like John Berryman's autobiographical character Henry in *The Dream Songs*, Lentricchia has a jittery, in-your-face patter that demands a response of some kind. He's a performer and an exhibitionist – in this book, literally – and he needs engagement with his audience. An angry response is better than no reaction at all: "When I'm doing this, whatever 'this' is, and that's not my problem, that's your problem, if you want that problem, which you don't have to have because nobody is holding a gun to your head and demanding that you tell us what this is, when I'm doing this . . ." And so forth.

This book demands a personal response and, frankly, I'm not crazy about this guy, the main character of the book. Among many other things, I don't like his confrontational posture. However, I like the way the actual person Frank Lentricchia takes current problems of subjectivity and responsibility that he has addressed in his theoretical and critical works and unabashedly acts them out. I like the fiction of presence in this book, the mutual agreement between the two of us that I will read those selves he projects as real characters. I like his struggle with issues of sincerity and authenticity:

> I'm acting a little, trying out a line a little. I like to act. As I say, What a shocking idea!, as I begin to propel the words from my mouth, as they start to skip off my tongue, I'm sincere, completely so, but as the sentence forms, when it's finished, I'm no longer sincere. I'm delivering a line, behind which I hide.

In a way, the whole book is an exploration of the

question, "Where shall your sincerity be located, in this theater of yourself?"

I like the way that, lacking a father and family tradition that he wants to rebel against in print, Lentricchia takes on T.S. Eliot, W.B. Yeats, and Wallace Stevens as surrogates with whom he can identify and also argue. Indeed, the book is best read as a counterpart to *Modernist Quartet*, his many-years-in-the-making study of Frost, Stevens, Pound, and Eliot. Anxiety of influence is much too mild a term to describe his engagement with, for example, "My Kinsman, T.S. Eliot" in both books. He claims and questions this kinship through his allusion to Eliot's *Four Quartets* in the title of the critical text as well as in countless references and appropriations and parodies throughout *The Edge of Night*. He is well aware of how ludicrous such a kinship might appear: "How would I explain that to my grandparents . . .? Eliot, my kinsman, from St. Louis, a premier WASP who went to Harvard, then to England for good, where he took on a different sound, like a complete Englishman. Absurd." But he knows one sure basis of their connection: "We both wanted to sound like somebody else . . . Theater as the medium of our kinship."

As he performs his way through *The Edge of Night*, Lentricchia repeatedly refers to Eliot's insistence on the extinction of personality, the poet's "continual surrender of himself as he is at the moment to something which is more valuable." In *Modernist Quartet*, he tellingly glosses a key term: "By 'personality' Eliot means something we possess painfully, in isolating individuality; and those who have a personality know what it means to want to escape it." Lentricchia, apparently saddled with a self that he wants desperately to escape, explores three avenues of liberation. First, there is writing. He quotes Eliot, who says that the writer experiences "a moment of exhaustion, of appeasement, of absolution, and of something very near annihilation, which is in itself indescribable." Lentricchia likes this. While writing, he says, "For once, you like yourself. The annihilation you experience is indescribably good, because it is the death of everything you were outside the process. The opaque burdens of your self-consciousness are lifted."

Reading, too, allows him to surrender self-consciousness. He recalls an early teacher's refusal to retell a story she had already told:

That's how I remember my first literary experience. I remember it not directly but by remembering the bad part whose badness was bad because of how different it was from the day before, when it must have been terrific, at the feet of Miss Beach, living in literature, which I don't remember, when I must have surrendered whatever self I

34

had to something more valuable, something alive in Miss Beach's voice.

Lentricchia frames this anecdote of literary experience in terms of a missing origin; his passionate surrender of self in literature "must have been terrific," he says, but he can't remember it. This uneasy affirmation of the joy of "living in literature" perhaps reflects the uncomfortable state of literary studies in the 1990s, when to confess that one loves to read poems or novels is suspect. In other parts of the text, however, Lentricchia confronts the issue head on. Reading *The Waste Land*, he is filled with "fierce joy." He "luxuriates" in his performance of the poem, while at the same time the "other, nonperforming 'I'" is trying futilely to write criticism about the text. All Lentricchia's books demonstrate his ability to lose himself in literature as well as his compulsion to annotate, to theorize, to reflect; in *The Edge of Night*, in a radical departure from the example of his earlier writing practices, he turns abstraction into the devil:

> Having sacrificed yourself to something more valuable . . . in the formal text of a poem, you are tempted to move above, in an effort to explain why you tell the stories you tell . . . Having yielded, having taken a vacation from who you are, having in a way forgotten yourself in order to find a more satisfying self, you begin to reflect on your

"position" and "allegiances" . . . The Devil of
Theory: you know him well.

The most unexpected path that Lentricchia
takes to the extinction of personality leads
through the gates of Mepkin Abbey, a monastery where he retreats on more than one occasion. Although Lentricchia says that he does
not believe in God, in this book the Roman
Catholic contemplative Thomas Merton becomes, with Eliot, a guiding genius of self-sur-
render. Lentricchia insists that "there is no
story adequate to what occurred during those
three days in late April of 1991. Mepkin Abbey
. . . will not yield to sly narrative method, or
maybe any other kind of method."
Nevertheless, in this book of narrative discontinuity, of personal anecdote that gives way to
reflection that gives way to posturing, his
account of this escape from the self reads more
smoothly than that of any other.

I sympathize with Lentricchia's desire for
the relief he feels at Mepkin Abbey. Because
when he emerges, as when he emerges from his
writing or his reading, he has to return not only
to that self he doesn't like but also to the frac-
tious world of academe – the world in which he
is a famous critic. The academy as a whole is
not likely to embrace this book, and despite
Random House's provocative packaging, it has

not been a big crossover hit either. It's a compelling performance, but it's hard to imagine its ideal audience.

On *Johnny Critelli* and *The Knifemen*

VINCE PASSARO

Frank Lentricchia may be the only person in America whose job description reads "ex-literary critic." This is like describing yourself as an ex-priest, only rarer and more dangerous. Shortly before his new book, a set of harmonizing novellas, *Johnny Critelli* and *The Knifemen* came out, Mr. Lentricchia, who teaches in Duke University's notoriously postmodern English department, took to the pages of *Lingua Franca*, an influential magazine for college professors, to renounce the bloodless profession he had once eagerly embraced as a prominent lit-theory bad boy and author of several works of literary and cultural criticism, most notably, *Criticism and Social Change* in 1983. His conversion, he says, came in a graduate class seven years ago while trying to fend off student assertions of racism and ethnocentricity in William Faulkner and Don DeLillo. "When I grew up and became a literary critic, I learned to keep silent about the reading experiences of liberation that I'd enjoyed since childhood," he tells us. He still teaches, he says, but only undergraduates, so that he can "talk to people who, like me, need to read great literature just as much as they need to eat."

Mr. Lentricchia finds himself in a relatively unusual position for a member of his former field: He can actually write imaginative works of literature. His first book of that sort, a memoir entitled *The Edge of Night*, received justifiably positive attention when it was published in 1994.

Now, his two novels arrive, nicely packaged by Scribner to give a hint, but only a hint, of the ominous material that lies between the covers.

It is not surprising that Mr. Lentricchia has had to give up any pretensions to a field that lately claims literature and its theoreticians can be agents of positive social change. His own heart, like those of most good writers, wants its own say; he is little interested in positive social change and seeks mostly painful memory and an atmosphere of violence and destruction. This puts him in good company, part of a powerful modern tradition – the literature of self-loathing, it might be called, constituted by an eclectic band of artists dating back to Laurence Sterne and Edgar Allan Poe, moving forward through Gustave Flaubert, Charles Baudelaire,

Oscar Wilde, Thomas Mann, T.S. Eliot and Nathaniel West, and reaching its apex with the likes of Henry Miller, Jean Genet, Celine, Charles Bukowski and William Burroughs.

The two stories reach back imaginatively to Mr. Lentricchia's youth in Utica, N.Y., where he grew up in what seems an intense and insulated Italian-American community. *Johnny Critelli*, which involves the Lentricchia family by name, is an impressionistic reworking of openly autobiographical material, centering on the mythical figure named in the title, a local hero, a friend of the working man and a union organizer. It is a kinder story than *The Knifemen*, which is more directly novelistic, with a strange and complexly revealed plot and a beautifully coherent symbolic structure. *The Knifemen* concerns the ironically named Richard Assisi, a popular obstetrician-gynecologist with a dark life of secret misogyny. When he's not on call, he watches real-time coverage of the O.J. Simpson trial, sympathizing with defendant, masturbating and eating Fig Newtons. He has a girlfriend but chases her off resolutely – finally, convincingly, with a knife. He got his start in medicine by participating in a particularly loathsome back-room abortion in the 1950s in Utica.

Both stories trawl the dark waters of manhood, desire and rage, and Mr. Lentricchia throws back none of the strange beasts he drags up from the deep. A few years back, an editor I know considered but did not publish Mr. Lentricchia's *The Edge of Night*. She later told me it had scared her. I took this to be a good sign for the book, which it was. *Johnny Critelli* and *The Knifemen* should scare people even more, so soaked are they in the rich odors of ancient blood and wretched impulses. *Johnny Critelli* has the more roseate glow of a loving, if difficult family at its core, but it, too, gets its coloration from what Mr. Lentricchia refers to as "traces of bloody melodrama." Conversations with the narrator's father take place with the murder scenes of great Italian operas playing on the radio in the background.

All three of Mr. Lentricchia's creative works so far display an obsession with manhood, with men and with the proximity that Italian men in particular seem to see between love and violence. "Okay. We take as a given he beat the shit out of them both," says the evil genius of *The Knifemen*, Victor Graziadei (the names are all loaded). Victor is the man who directs Richard Assisi toward his current profession, as well as toward his debilitating fantasies. The conversation concerns an earlier hero, pre-O.J. Simpson – Johnny Stompanato, Lana Turner's lover, who was murdered by Turner's fourteen-year-old daughter. Gone but never forgotten.

It is this Victor Graziadei who introduces the young Richard Assisi to the ways of the knife, in the slaughterhouse as well as the back alley, taking him in as he would an acolyte into a secret cult of manhood. They sit together over pastry. "We are who we are, true or false?" Victor asks an embarrassed eighteen-year-old Richard. "He paused for a long time, his eyes still on me, mine trying to focus on the espresso. Then he said, 'With men who enjoy each other's company, these awkward moments are traditional. After a point, you learn to accept the pain. You learn to love it.' Victor said 'men.'" A scorching and hurtful sense of intimacy rules these men's lives. The conversation with Victor resonates with a scene in *Johnny Critelli* where Mr. Lentricchia, imagining Christ in the garden with the apostles sleeping nearby, writes, "Jesus needs the company of his close friends who are all men. Try not to extract sexual implications and I'll be grateful. The proximity of males is necessary for males. The vicinity, the shelter of males."

Such scenes recur, with fathers, with uncles, with other men, Italian men at the table, particularly in the clean-tiled Italian pastry shops, men using their fine motor controls, eating and sipping with delicate fingers while murmuring of violence.

There is a similar scene in *The Edge of Night*, also in a pastry shop. This is Mr. Lentricchia's motivating force, his central moral dilemma, and he makes it vivid and compelling almost against our will, which is one of the signs that an artist, not a critic, is at work.

He Sings the Body Tinterotic

JODY MCAULIFFE

*The bodies of men and women engirth me, and I
    engirth them,
They will not let me off nor I them till I go with
    them and respond to them
and love them.*

Walt Whitman,
"I Sing the Body Electric"

When I am asked by the novelist, as I invariably am from time to time not simply because the novelist is my husband, but because I was present at the conception – which is my favorite of his novels? – my answer, after a momentary reflection, is always *Johnny Critelli*. Why *Johnny Critelli*, he wants to know, though I can tell he's secretly pleased. Because I have involvement with *Johnny Critelli* – not with the man himself, but with the process of the novel that bears his name. Because it is a novel of process and I am a theater director concerned with and compelled by process. And, of course, because of the writing. The title suggests familiarity, as in member of the family, the novel stemming from an image of Critelli surrounded by key members of Frank's family. Young Frank heard the Depression era story of Johnny Critelli told again and again around the Lentricchia family dinner table, where grandfathers Augusto and Tommaso and Uncles Bill (a.k.a. Goody), Dom (a.k.a. Doom), and Frank's father Frank (no a.k.a.) regularly assembled, wives in tow in ethnic Utica, New York. To appreciate *Johnny Critelli*, you have to ask yourself not simply who, but what is Critelli: Frank's spiritual uncle, his father, his secret self. It's a secret trinity like the other Trinity where one suffers so that others can go free.

This is a novel born from an image from that old family story, an image from Frank's memory, the kind of image that you have to wonder, did it really happen or did he dream it? How does it become part of Lentricchia family mythology? Frank fixes on the image, and he wants to make it move. Since I'm a theater director, I suggest that he treat it as a frame of a movie: it could be an opening image, a central image, or the final image of a sequence; he can spin the time backwards or forwards away from or toward this central image. How do they get here and where do they go next? Unravel the movie frame by frame: imagine the narrative like a storyboard. Initiate the reader into Lentricchian tradition.

It's all in "the context of the telling, usually at the dinner table, that's where all the fun was." And it's sixteen-year-old Frank in the novel who's asking "What did Uncle Bill say Johnny Critelli did in that saloon?" – delighted to see his father pleased that he's brought it up. And Frank then, and now, tells it:

One night, in a saloon, Uncle Bill said a drunk walked in and threw up on the floor. He must have just eaten because you could see little pieces of meat and carrot. It was a nice stew, Uncle Bill said. And Johnny Critelli said, For five bucks I'll take two slices of bread and make a sandwich. I'll mop it up. Somebody put up the five bucks and Johnny Critelli took two slices of bread and mopped it up, he made a soggy sandwich, the stuff is hanging and dripping out, like long strings of white snot, and he eats it all.

Why, you might well ask, does Johnny eat the vomit sandwich and why do the Lentricchias have to talk about it at the dinner table? Not for money; in fact, it's the one who vomits and the Brothers Lentricchia who get paid. In lieu of payment, Johnny spins his own extreme version of Mark's Gospel, Chapter Seven, about how vomit is clean, as anything that goes into the stomach and passes into the sewer is clean. Maybe this is why they always tell it at the table – when people are eating. Evil, the source of

46

uncleanliness, comes from within, from the heart. The Brothers talk about the money until Johnny, at the end of the novel, interrupts them and convinces Uncle Bill – the middle son and director of this spectacle – to tell the story of their lives: "Do this in memory of us all." The last line echoing Christ's at the last Supper contains the beginning of the circular novel.

Frank's Critelli is Utica's idiot savant, the simpleton artist, the Fool to the patriarch Augusto Lentricchia's Lear. His homeless holy fool and "godly man of rags" goes around in a Harlequin coat emitting Tinterotic chiaroscuro. (Tinterotic as in recognizing the erotic element in Tintoretto's religious paintings.) Johnny's a live painting – speaking in riddles, prophesying, disrupting, and challenging. Frank sneaks the Christ narrative under the Critelli image and he has his contrapposto. Is Critelli's madness real or simulated? Is he divinely inspired? He writes the truth to Augusto the father, that his sons cannot see or say, in a spectacular line: "Signor Augusto, You are wrong about everything," and signs his name John, not Johnny, because this is serious. Destitution of emotion must be Augusto's great crime, that and his silence. And Augusto's grandson, Frank the author, speaks the truth of that to us, in richly emotional, heavenly crazy prose.

In the beginning there is baseball: *Johnny in*

the Park, the prologue. *Johnny Critelli* begins, not with the standard narrative device, the once upon a time: "It was the summer of 1956 and he was sixteen." That's the fourth line of the novel, because Frank is pitching a different ballgame. He opens with a curve ball: "Naturally, at the time, he was bored, and he saw nothing." He is sixteen-year-old Frank and he's in the park where he takes his grandmother to pick dandelions. Boredom is natural. It is the natural state of mind of Lefty, a.k.a. Frank Lentricchia. Boredom causes Lefty to see nothing and Lefty sees nothing because he's bored. The nickname – Lefty – followed by a question mark because who is he really? In his radical days, left-handed Frank even sported a license plate, "GO LEFT." "People had trouble remembering his name" – Lefty or Frank? Frank wants people to remember him, but he wants deliverance from his own past. He wants to forget everything – the boring Italians from Utica and this green park, their domain after all. Frankie, his grandmother calls him. She remembers him, she remembers his name. Believing he's remembering is as natural as boredom, and through the Hollywood shades of his younger, nascent-aesthetic self, Tinterotic-sensualistic Frank sees the image of his grandmother, bending over picking greens, multiplied all over his field of vision – "great rounded

48

asses," "endless breasts," "curving bodies" – as in a painting by Magritte.

The park is also the site of a Little League baseball game. Frank, the writer, remembers his sixteen-year-old self remembering himself at twelve, a child of many fathers and only one father, pitching before two men watching the game from the bleachers: his father and the man in the mirrored sunglasses – the title character, the hero, J.C., Johnny Critelli. Critelli's opacity, his reflectivity, becomes the camera lens for Frank's personal movie, the narrative of his autobiography. Frank reflects on himself projected in J.C.'s penetrating gaze. On the pitcher's mound, the artist inside Frank struggles to emerge. Johnny, the shadow father, sees through young Frankie to the self within the body of the pitcher on the mound, spasming in athletic labor as he struggles to birth his true self, his artistic self. Johnny's mystical power consists of his ability to transcend the body, to ascend, to assume Frank into a heaven of artistic expression:

> Johnny Critelli feels himself urged by a cause unknown to float out and rush down upon the kid in gentle breezy force, this is the urge, to rush out of himself and soar down upon him, the boy of the spasms, and to lift him up and out . . .

This artistic Assumption is directly akin to the moment when the athlete loses himself in a spectacular feat. Frankie's spasming body is in conflict with his own staring concentration and his stiff actual father Frank sitting in the stands for once watching. What is the thing besides a winning pitch that's trying to jump out of Frankie's body? Is it this book?

What makes Johnny want to lift Frankie out of himself? Frank suggests that it's because Johnny's seen enough intensity in the world. Johnny assumes Frankie out of his body and lifts his father's gaze so high above the field that he can't see his son's athletic imperfection. But the paradox is that the one hit in the almost no hitter game that Frankie the pitcher gives up is "the most beautiful thing in the world." He loses but he wins: he creates the kind of beauty that requires imperfection. The spasm of athletic labor reveals Critelli as Frank's muse and now Frank, at last, can see to write: "Remembrance is better, even when it's worse it's better, this remembrance of things that never were as I remember them."

In this novel-as-theater, Frank views and reviews what he remembers. It's not only fiction because he's not making it up and the characters live and die outside the text. It's midnight opera, and Frank the writer assumes the reader into heavenly musical transport with orgiastic cascades of words. The Italian predecessor of this late night enterprise is Luigi Pirandello, whose maid/muse called Fantasy wears a cap and bells much like Lentricchia's Critelli. She visits a family onto Pirandello and *Six Characters in Search of an Author* is the result. The image of Critelli eating the vomit sandwich off the barroom floor provides the occasion for Critelli to bring into Lentricchia's study all the members of his family: his father and uncles – the Brothers Lentricchia; his grandfathers; his mother and the companion (me). This is the story of their adventures: they shout and project their passions in Frank's face. They're as alive to us as to Frank, real people who do not want to become characters. The companion (read me) pleads their case:

> How long have you known that we are rehearsing *Six Characters in Search of an Author*? It could not have been otherwise. The woman in Florida and I, and all the rest, we're human beings in the making, in flight from an author who wants to turn us into characters. Ignore his protestations to the contrary, this is his relentless intention, to make us textual puppets.

Pirandello distinguishes between historical writers interested only in the pleasure of narration and philosophical writers in the grip of a spiritual need. Both Pirandello and Frank fall into this latter category. Seeking in the image of Critelli, wild and free, a meaning to give value to the central image, Frank turns the act of writing into transubstantiation. Critelli does a necessary thing – he eats the vomit sandwich off the barroom floor on a bet. The Lentricchian Last Supper, Frank's musing on all that preceded it, and the celebration of that moment in tales at the dinner table form a religious rite in a heretical Christianity (read Critellianity) of literary obsession. Critelli really eats the vomit, but Frank's fantasy creates the rest of Critelli's life. Everything's in motion; it's a sudden experiment, a true romance: "Eat them with these sentences. They die while you write the book, while you're writing. Eat these sentences, these are their bodies. The last supper is a supper of sentences. The only supper."

So this is writing about writing, and writing about eating, and writing about eating writing. Forget so-called dinner theater, this is eating theater. The key images from memory explode in recurrent verbal frescoes as vivid as Tintoretto's paintings on the dark walls of his Scuola Grande di San Rocco in Venice: tumultuous scenes of Christ's Passion. Here are the scenes that make up the life of Lentricchia: the midnight sandwiches with his father, the moment his father flings him – a child – across a room, the secret desire of Uncle Bill ("Goody") to be his father, the deepest need for stories to make sense out of a life – Christ's or Critelli's, or Christ's through Critelli's, or Critelli's through Christ's.

In the first section of three, *Fathers*, Frank leaps back and forth from the images of the past to the images of the present with the companion (me) in an obsessive effort to disappear into a radical story-stew, marrying image and writing. What emerges is a unique novelistic form, a lyric struggle to shape the images into a romance. Hawthorne, in his Preface to *The House of Seven Gables*, articulates the difference between the novel and the romance:

> When a writer calls his work a romance . . . he wishes to claim a certain latitude which he would not have felt himself entitled to assume had he professed to be writing a novel. The latter form of composition is presumed to aim at a very minute fidelity to the probable and ordinary course of man's experience. The former – while it sins unpardonably so far as it may swerve aside from the truth of the human heart – has fairly a right to present that truth under circumstances, to a great extent, of the writer's own choosing or creation. If he think it fit, also, he may so manage his atmospherical medium as to bring out or mellow the lights and deepen and enrich the shadows of the picture.

Hawthorne here anticipates Frank's original approach to his autobiographical material: he does not aim at fidelity to the probable or ordinary experience; quite the contrary, he chooses and creates extraordinary circumstances. Though Frank really did perform Tintoretto's Baptism in the middle of the night in Venice, wearing a loincloth in an elegant, overheated room in the Gabrielli-Sandwirth Hotel on the street of slaves, overlooking the Laguna Veneta, his evocation of that experience is romantic, as Hawthorne defines the term, in its primary adherence to the truth of Frank's heart. Every bite of life is grist for the mill of his heated imagination. The companion speaks:

> I remember my friend best in Venice. Invaded by Tintoretto's force. . . He did the expected scenes, the crucifixion and so forth. But the Virgin in her Assumption? I was touched by the lightness and the modesty. Can you imagine his Annunciation? His shy reception of the angel? Roles assumed and discarded in seconds, one after the other in a makeshift loincloth, doing even those nameless bystanders of the Christian Theater at the edges of paintings. So many in an obscure light. He was shocked back by the agony and glow of transfigured flesh, so many burly bodies – his too – becoming balletic, dancing his awe, in Venice. [*She pauses.*] It's a beautiful sound and a summons. Critelli, the secret of Venice. He's chasing Critelli.

Johnny eats the vomit so that the Brothers Lentricchia, and therefore the grandson, can live. The "shelter of males" is necessary for this mira-

54

cle. Family photographs fuel Frank's imaginative memory. The photograph that hung in our dining room for years but is now inexplicably banished to the laundry room (because it has served its purpose?), occasions another meditation: the Brothers as children, pregnant like the pitcher on the mound with their grown-up selves; the photo of Augusto, the writer, and his friend Silverio becomes an image from a theatrical scene on the eve of the taking of the photo of the three Brothers Lentricchia as children. Augusto plays Othello and Silverio Desdemona for Augusto's wife's enjoyment. As in the moment on the pitcher's mound, Frank's father – a child – leaps out of himself with joy into the adult scene, wanting to play, too, but Augusto meets him with lonely vacancy, with nothingness. What we see is a child full of expressivity who's consigned to a spiritual death by his father's emotional absence. And in the photo of the three brothers taken the next day, Frank Senior's gaze veers off camera, drawn to a photo of Big Bill Tilden (the great American tennis star of the 1920s) on the wall of the photographer's studio – he's on a long journey to his own interior, in flight from his father's coldness and yearning for the sublime. Though Frank, too, was met with absence, he finds his expressivity and spiritual vitality: writing spells escape from paternal ice.

Johnny Critelli is, in many ways, a love song to Frank's father's interior, a way of discovering his father's undiscovered country. In concretizing his father's interior life, Frank imaginatively articulates his father's love of tennis. Big Bill Tilden becomes Tinterotic, too, and the image of Big Bill, "this flowing killer, this heavy-jawed angel," lets Frank the father escape death a little because that's what sports and art can do for us. "We have art," Nietzsche says, "so that we shall not be destroyed by the truth." Frankie the pitcher grasps Tilden's tennis and he gets a little closer to his father. At the end of the first section, Frank assembles his cast (including Uncle Doom's cock) in the saloon ready to hear Johnny's gospel, upstaged by the miracle of Doom's glorious coming.

In the second section, *Companions*, Frank's two women take center stage in alternating monologues. All the women in this tale – Johnny's mother, Frank's mother, and the companion – are tough, but Frank's mother's voice, created, naturally, by Frank, erupts with defiance. She even suggests that the core story of Critelli in the bar is made up, just another product of Bill's fartistry. She remembers Bill fondly as an artist of farting, dancing and playing with what she calls his "moon voice." I call Bill a fartist because my job, in life, as in the novel, is

to pun. Frank's mother insists on her own existence and refuses the control of her author son.
She is the mother, after all. The companion, the
tall Irish girl who's supposed to be Irish is supposed to be me. My other job is to play Ezra
Pound to Frank's Eliot, to facilitate cinema-lov-
ing Frank to make his novel of images. The central image of this section is his mother's story of
her miscarriage – the child she lost – and her
desire still to have another child even in her sev-
enties; her suffering at the loss of her child and
her desire for Frank to make her a baby. What
Frank can make her is writing – here so full of
heartbreak mixed inextricably with sardonic
humor – and she figures that since he's making
half of their lives up he can make the image of a
baby for her. Frank makes her story rough with
grief and resilient humor, and she can put it on
top of her television set with all his other books
or "ball peen hammer" it somewhere where the
sun don't shine.

Frank exorcises his extremity on the page, in
literature, in images of family where he is truly
loved, writing like an actor possessed of his role,
invaded by Tintoretto's force. Tinteroticism,
paradoxically, is also asceticism and Frank's
experience of art is spiritual as well as sensual. In
the third and final section, *Augusto*, we meet
Critelli as a boy of ten, drawn to his friend

Augusto as Frank was drawn to his paternal grandfather. Though a southern Italian, Augusto bears the marks of the chilly, austere, mountainous, reasonable north. And against this force, Frank sets his maternal grandfather's hot rage and humor, and Johnny's enthusiasm: reason vs. passion. In *Johnny Critelli*, Frank absorbs both grandfathers – Tommaso the Italian clown, the teller of obscene tales, and Augusto the American writer, the political poet – into his blood. Dueling monologists Augusto – coldly angry, absent, pleasurably unhappy – and Critelli – passionate, present, simple – fight to the finish: Critelli's note to Augusto that he's "wrong about everything" is the knockout blow. It's a Beckettian Italianate opera. Enter Augusto's friend Silverio and Tommaso, and Frank paints these men, artists of life, devouring Michelangelo and Leonardo, then taking a nap after their huge meal of words and images just like the Apostles after the Last Supper in Tintoretto's surprising rendering that hangs in Venice, in the church of San Trovaso. Silverio says, " . . . this *Last Supper* is a scandal . . . This *Last Supper* is wonderful": "An apostle passed out on the table, his hair in the food, another reaching for the jug of wine on the floor behind him and trying to look at Christ at the same time. What was that smear on the floor? *Gesu Cristo* in a saloon, with his eyes going up to the ceiling, drunk like the rest of those bums."

Frank concludes with his oldest memory: the last great aria a conflation of Tintoretto's *Last Supper* and, at last, the culminating tale of Johnny Critelli in the saloon. He writes like his Christ walks on water (a fleshy Christ with stinky, crusty feet) because it's his gift, because he loves his gift, because he enjoys doing it, he just loves it, giving birth to the Brothers Lentricchia and, in the process, himself. He won't drown. And the reader gets to walk on water with him. "Even our lives are good enough for a little story." At the end, we must begin again. "Start the story! Do this in memory of us all."

The ultimate goal of Frank's writing is self-forgetfulness – the gift of not thinking – but in order to forget yourself you must remember. Johnny's advice: "Throw away your memories after you write them. Maybe this is a moral." In the pages of this book, Frank makes a shelter for his soul wherein he's connected to his deepest self. Inside the novel, he's protected by his family and loved ones in the photographs, in the fabricated memories, and, above all, in his imagination, soaring with Johnny.

Lentricchia's Gangsters

FRED GARDAPHE

In *The Music of the Inferno*, Frank Lentricchia presents Robert Tagliaferro, an orphaned child of unknown racial background, who makes a grim discovery of the corpse of a young child, which he respectfully buries shortly after his eighteenth birthday then flees his hometown of Utica, New York; and takes refuge in a bookstore in New York City, where he reads his way through the shelves: "In the absence of a father, I acquired knowledge. My knowledge is my memory." Robert's character becomes a composite of all that he has absorbed through his studies. Along the way he keeps notebooks "containing in a minute script illegible to all but himself the fruits of forty-two years of research in the history of Utica and New York State, from the coming of the Dutch to the present." In those notebooks, Robert fortifies himself with knowledge he will need to overcome the gangsters of his past.

The one thing that Robert is not is sexual. There is no information about his past sexual encounters. He is familiar with human sexuality, but it is hard to tell if it is knowledge gained solely from reading or talking rather than actual experience. Robert returns to Utica at age forty-two, under the pseudonym Robert Forza, to uncover the town's secrets through his knowledge and memory.

The sights conjured in Lentricchia's literary inferno are gruesome and, like those in the great work of Dante, are directly connected to the sinners' actions. The novel presents a vision of darkness that is as exhilarating as it is disturbing; it is the destruction, if not the deconstruction, of the mafioso prototype, and the destroyer is the intellectual, "this curious man, all made of words." Robert has become the cultural critic who has the power to undo wrongs of the past by forcing men to confront their evil deeds. A man who knows the past, who knows what has been erased, repressed, or forgotten, can be a very dangerous man, especially when he has been hurt by those who created the history he has studied. Robert sees himself as "an ethnic freak in this fair city of such clear ethnic divisions," who has "come back to return the pain."

Going home can be hell, and in this revision of returning home, Lentricchia penetrates the dark recesses of a Little Italy to reveal the sins of Utica's "immigrant merchant princes" who shaped the city's economy, and thus its history. Robert, returned home, begins to change everyone's sense of Utica's past. He meets Alex Lucas, whose name should have been Alessandro Lucca, the great-great-grandson of one of the original Italian immigrants to Utica. Alex's ancestor shamed the family enough to make them change their name. Lucas, who in many ways stands to benefit from Robert's knowledge, helps Robert connect to the town's leading Italians. He secures Robert an invitation to the regular dinner meeting of a group which includes men like Albert Cesso and Sebastian Spina, descendants of Utica's first Italian immigrants. These contemporary power brokers meet in the cellar of a restaurant with a gangster boss named Joseph "Our Mother" Paternostra: "slim, spry, ninety years old . . . Never called or referred to as 'Our Mother' within earshot, except once. A major mafia *capo* who had controlled for almost sixty-five years the Utica-Syracuse area on behalf of the Don of all Upstate New York (with the exception of that peculiar toilet: Albany)." For most of the novel, Paternostra's sexual orientation remains unclear. Yet when Alex first tells Robert about the town leaders, Robert says that Alex's characterization of the men suggests that "I'd stumbled upon a ring of homosexual gangsters."

Lentricchia debunks the traditional sexuality of the gangster through the figure of Paternostra, the gay mafioso; the racism of Italian Americans through the figure of racist alderman Sebastian Spina, a mayoral candidate; and the pomposity of professionalism through dentist Albert Cesso and Louis Ayoub, a professor of literature, music and art, who is writing a book entitled, *The Music of the Inferno*. Most of these town leaders have an ancestral link to the founding myths of Utica's Little Italy, and in many ways this is a story about the end of a Little Italy and about how book learning helps to end that world and preserve it at the same time. It is also about the place of modernism in a postmodern world, about the role of facts in history, the purpose of ethnic identity, and the role storytelling plays in claiming and naming that history. The various encounters of Robert and the town leaders in the inferno of Joe's restaurant, where Robert tells his stories over a series of dinners, rewrite the hells of Dante and Milton into the hell of Jean-Paul Sartre, so that "hell" becomes the way the past rests in one's mind after it has been delivered there through other people. Redemption happens only through the revolutionary act of revising the past without reliving it. Robert's dinners, in a sense, represent the afterlife where the gangster awaits the judgement – here, from the cultural critic Robert Tagliaferro. By running away from home as a young man and educating himself, Robert has transformed himself from potential wiseguy into a wise man.

Robert first attacks the gangster image by invoking the Madonna with the phrase "Our Mother." Everyone in the story knows how Paternostra got the nickname "Our Mother," and that to use it in public is to signal a death wish because it questions the man's masculinity in front of other men. Robert uses the phrase during the retelling of the first sighting of the bay of Manhattan by Dutch explorers, for whom the vision echoes the "originating instant of Greek mythology, the divinization of the earth. The god of all gods, preceding all gods, was a goddess. She was Our Mother, whose womb swelled as the Virgin Mary's would, and from her came everything good, including Our Father, who was questionable." When Professor Ayoub accuses Robert of getting away with speaking "the unspeakable" and of knowing the story of Paternostra's nickname, Robert replies, "A curious footnote, Professor, buried deep in a famous book of the 1960s on the Mafia." Then Robert suggests that Paternostra might suspect that Ayoub knows the truth, but that Paternostra is "a fool beyond our comprehension" because he harbors the "tremendous illusion" that Ayoub is "[t]he man of intellect. The man who has never been fondled by the desire for power" and is, therefore, no threat to Paternostra's power. It is at this point that the reader is finally given the whole story.

As the story goes, Paternostra is running a high-stakes craps game that has been held up a couple of times. He stops by to ensure its security and while he is there, it is held up again. The robber points the gun at Paternostra and has him strip naked. When he does, Paternostra with "no tone in his pectorals" reveals he has womanlike breasts. The robber responds, "Now you know why Mr. Big Shot is called 'Our Mother' behind his back." Then the robber orders Paternostra's bodyguard, Rosario, to suck on his boss's breast, and when he does, Paternostra achieves an erection and ejaculates. Thus, the nickname is born.

By retelling the story, Robert debunks the traditional macho power behind which the gangster hides and not only reveals the gangster's weakness but also asserts the power of the intellectual to overcome that of the wiseguy. But more than this, Paternostra maintains a homosexual relationship with his blond weight-lifter companion. Robert later explains to Alex that "Joseph Paternostra was the Old Don's catamite, a Queen of the Mafia." In this way, Lentricchia turns the homosocial world of the Mafia askew and gives it a glint of homosexuality, undermining its traditional and apparently superficial heterosexual foundation.

Lentricchia, in a truly postmodern move, disrupts Mario Puzo's master gangster narrative. In a direct reference to Puzo's *The Godfather*, the men allude to Puzo as they discuss the founding fathers of Utica:

Ayoub: "Behind every great family lies a crime."
Paternostra: "And a politician."
Alex: "And eventually a writer."

The allusion is to the Balzac quote that Puzo's uses as an epigraph to his novel, something that is pointed out by the Professor, who goes on: "Remembered in the lineage of all the great families, legitimate and illegitimate, in the womb of the crime, the United States of Mafia. All wealth is guilty at the source." When accused by the gangster Paternostra of exaggerating everything, Ayoub responds: "The road of exaggeration leads to the palace of fact. Yes, the homeopathic imagination of Mario Puzo, the splendid luridness of his instincts, whose ancestors hid the meaning of their surname by dropping the second 'z,' Mario the novelist with a nose for the disguised stench of all great families. Puzo?

Puzzo: Stink." Robert goes on to tell the stories of Utica's founding fathers and how they stole their fortunes, to which Ayoub responds:

> "Mario the Stinker has already told your story of swindlers, Mr. Forza, and made a fortune doing so."
> Robert: "As did Mr. Faulkner before him."
> Ayoub: "Yes."
> Robert: "As did Mr. Fitzgerald before Mr. Faulkner."
> Ayoub: "Yes. The American literary history of family gangsterism."

Their litany reveals the connection between American literature and the male powers of history that have come and gone before the Italian gangster.

Along with taking down the gangster in this novel, Lentricchia takes a whack at the silly chauvinism that often accompanies public displays of ethnic pride. Robert also attacks Spina, a racist who may be guilty of murder in the past; the victim of which Robert believes is hidden under Spina's driveway. Spina represents "blood pride" – a kind of mindless glorying in his identity as an Italian. Robert plans to open an investigation into Spina's past once Spina has been elected mayor of Utica, for he believes "Italian-American pride needs the forum and status of the mayoralty. A great victory comes before the fall." What follows is a series of mock responses given out by Alex and Robert:

> "We are virtuous, because we are Italian."
> "We will support and love each other because we are Italian."
> "It's a privilege to be fucking Italian."
> "I honor you, my Italian friend, though your values disgust me."
> "The Italian-American people are a very great fucking people."
> "The ascension of Spina will trigger epic Italian-American self-cleansing. They will loathe their ethnicity. They will all want to change their surnames to Windsor, Spencer, or Bowles."

Here Lentricchia clears the air of the mindless ethnic boosterism that often pervades the Italian-American identity, especially when ethnic identity is based not on knowledge, but on feelings passed from one generation to the next. Lentricchia subtly introduces a possible antidote to this behavior by recognizing the power that art can have. Alex gives Robert a two-handled burial urn that stands about two feet tall. It is to contain the ashes of Robert's stepfather, Morris. They analyze the urn and discuss its relation to the first representation of the Madonna and Child and the origins of art:

> "25,000 B.C. The primal sculptor. He who needs to venerate in mimetic homage the one incontrovertible creative principle. It's the origin of art.

The male who needs."

"This has been said before."

"Yes, for 25,000 years. The male emerges from the mother, then spends the remainder of his life trying to represent the mother. A mama's boy. A sissy. *In utero*, forget genital difference. *In utero*, total femaleness. On this earth, when at last male, he walks but briefly, to and fro, in terrible independence from nature. Don't fuck with me! I am a man! In death, only the female. Back inside her oblivion. Secured forever from tumbling forth. Promise redeemed. Nature. God."

One of the ways a wiseguy becomes a wise man is to contemplate and incorporate aspects of what is traditionally considered female, always at the risk of losing a traditional sense of what is masculine.

At the final dinner, Robert continues his history of Utica, reaching the ancestors of Alex and Cesso and uncovering the sins of their families' past. A fire cuts the meal short and the men run for their lives. Robert takes off for parts unknown, a la Huck Finn, leaving his fortune to Alex. In many respects, Robert Tagliaferro, who has enacted his vendetta by coming "back to return the pain," plays the role of John the Baptist for the coming of the wise man to Italian-American literature. He uses his knowledge both to uncover the macho masquerade enacted by the traditional men of Utica's Little Italy and to right the wrongs of the past. He serves as a moral compass to counter the unchecked behavior of the gay gangster Joseph Paternostra and the crooked politician Sebastian Spina.

In his next novel, *Lucchesi and The Whale* (2001), Lentricchia defies traditional and commercial fiction. *Lucchesi and The Whale* is really an anti-narrative – tough reading, but rewarding for the reader familiar with American literature. In his acknowledgments, Lentricchia points to a few academic studies, novels by Don DeLillo, and Herman Melville's *Moby-Dick* as sources of inspiration for his new, macabre tale of a strange academic's search for truth. This section focuses on a small part of the novel which depicts a chance encounter between a gangster who has a name quite similar to that of the novel's protagonist and the protagonist himself.

The center of the fiction is Thomas Lucchesi, an academic wrapped up in his writing. Lucchesi talks mostly to himself, and when he does speak to others, it is as though he is lecturing. This character is a version of a figure common in Lentricchia's fiction: a man alone in the world. Lucchesi observes the fractured bits of his life as they crash into one another, as though seeing his world through a kaleidoscope. This work is among the best of what can be called "anti-novels." There is no plot; this brief (113 pages) fiction is no page-turner. Although it cannot be called a novel, it is a novel approach to writing fiction. What Lentricchia offers is writing that liberates the reader from the tugging leash of a plot. This writing is a story in itself.

Thomas Lucchesi is a man with a peculiar condition: he is with book, as a pregnant woman is with child. When he can't write, he can't breathe, and that is when he seeks inspiration in the strangest places. Sometimes he finds it at the bedside of the dying, mostly his close friends, but he'll take any dying acquaintance in a pinch. By confronting others' deaths, he denies, if not defies, his own, and in that moment gains enough power to fuel a few writing sessions. In the section in question, "High Blood Pleasure," the origins of Lucchesi the artist are presented. This section also includes a wild "sit-down" with the gangster Thomas "Three Finger Brown" Lucchese, who functions as the artist's distorted reflection in an ethnic mirror.

The story of how one writer named Tommy Lucchesi comes to meet one gangster, Gaetano "Tommy Three Finger Brown" Lucchese, is told by Geoffrey Gilbert, a friend of the protagonist who is marrying a female relative of the gangster. Gilbert portrays Lucchese, a year away from dying of a brain tumor, "like a character they called in Shakespearean times a fantastic, a more or less foppish person, who was more or less a homosexual," although he goes on to suggest that Lucchese was probably not a homosexual himself. The two Tommys meet in the gangster's hotel room. The writer has learned "everything there is to know about Three Finger Brown," and he sees the gangster as a "hidden muse" of his dark writings. Lucchesi the writer was "an English major who wrote stories full of violence in a poetic style" and authored such piquant phrases as "the eviscerations of friendship," "the ice-pick of conversation," "the blood-gouts of time," and "the lacerations of family." In contrast, Lucchese the gangster "actually did violence."

Gilbert and Lucchesi prepare for the meeting by researching the gangster's biography. They come to the realization that none of their research can be discussed with the gangster, who "had done 32 murders by the time he was 35." They meet in the hotel room while Three Finger is watching *The Arthur Godfrey Show* on television. The gangster asks the writer about his "plans for life," to which Lucchesi replies, "I want to be a writer." Lucchese responds that he does "a little writing in my domain, so I sympathize with what you have to go through," and then asks the writer to name some writers he idolizes. When Lucchesi says "John (the Lung)

Keats," nicknaming the poet with an allusion to his tuberculosis, the gangster says, "I heard of him, but we never met." They go on to talk about Keats's sexuality. The writer suggests that Keats was without a doubt heterosexual. The gangster replies, "an associate of mine once told me that art and sucking cock go hand-in-hand." This response is a defense of the masculinity that the gangster represents. Lucchese is in love with the "mouse," or girlfriend, of another gangster, Sam "Momo" Giancana, and she appears on television during the sit-down. Lucchese openly pines for her in front of the other two men. Soon Gilbert and Lucchesi are introduced to the gangster's bodyguard, a 547-pound man called Frank the Whale. "Three Finger Brown" Lucchese then pulls a move that he suggests is the reason for his nickname. The Whale explains that having only three fingers was a handicap that the gangster turned into an asset when he put them up rivals' asses to "dig around in there for the truth."

As in most of Lentricchia's fiction, a dark side emerges in *Lucchesi and The Whale*. Like Edgar Allan Poe, Lentricchia is fascinated with the grotesque, and *Lucchesi* takes us deep into that concept. The scene where the writer meets the gangster is telling in that it shows that educated men and gangsters, wise men and wiseguys, can sometimes be opposite sides of the same coin.

The writer Lucchesi has his whale, too – Melville's novel about a whale occupies, indeed obsesses, his experimental novel-in-progress about *Moby-Dick*. The gangster Lucchese has his whale, the 547-pound bodyguard. Their respective whales protect both men from harm that might come from the real world, a world over which they have little control. The whale becomes the only way to protect someone who has taken supernormal risks. Lucchesi the writer risks his career (and loses his teaching job) when he writes his "secrets in public print." He does not enjoy life outside the page. Lucchese the gangster risks losing a normal life by becoming a murderer, and he cannot enjoy life outside the world of gangsters. Lucchesi the writer advises his students to "live like a no-holds-barred autobiography of yourself, hide nothing so that you'll be freed for serious writing." Lucchese the gangster enacts the experiences that Lucchesi the writer wants without "the consequences." The writer secretly emulates the gangster, but he does not want to live with the possible consequences of a gangster's acts.

Lentricchia's Melville Troubles

THOMAS HOVE

In Lentricchia's recent writings, Herman Melville has become a thematic placeholder for various ideas about the intersections of art, domestic life, paternity, and violence. Lentricchia's tribute to Melville, *Lucchesi and The Whale* (2001), was his third book of fiction. He made the transition from academic criticism to creative writing in *The Edge of Night* (1994), which he followed up with two short novels in *Johnny Critelli* and *The Knifemen* (1996). His subsequent novel, *The Music of the Inferno* (1999), has the most conventional and compelling narrative drive of all his fictions. In these earlier works, Lentricchia would cite the occasional Melville reference, and his pale, monomaniac protagonist in *The Music of the Inferno* bears several resemblances to Ahab, Ishmael, and Bartleby. But in *Lucchesi and The Whale*, Lentricchia puts Melville at center stage to investigate the powers and dilemmas of writing, and the affinities between the artist and the orphan. In his life, Melville was a son abandoned by "an immortally problematic father." But in his writing, he is the "deliberate" orphan, the artist who sets himself against a hostile, overpowering environment dominated by politics and economics.

Lentricchia's narrator is a Melville enthusiast and novelist manqué named Thomas Lucchesi. As in his other fictions, Lentricchia uses Melville to explore a variety of love-hate relations between parents and children – what Lucchesi calls "the lacerations of family." One of the epigraphs to *The Music of the Inferno* comes from Chapter 114 of *Moby-Dick* ("The Gilder"): "Our souls are like those orphans whose unwedded mothers die in bearing them: the secret of our paternity lies in their grave, and we must there to learn it." To Lucchesi, this search for paternity is the primary impulse behind both Melville's and his own writing. *Moby-Dick* represents "nothing less than an abandoned son's (a son's, it is enough to say a son's) final retort to the voids of the Father God, voids flowing from the unbottomed reservoir of His Fatherly Nothingness." These familiar Freudian themes appear much more overtly in Melville's follow-up to *Moby-Dick*, the unjustly ignored *Pierre; or, The Ambiguities* (1852). But Lucchesi is most interested in relating their development in *Moby-Dick* to his own anxieties of authorial influence, as well as his yearning for contact with everyday life. A deliberate orphan like Melville, Lucchesi sees writing as "self-fathering," even "self-resurrection." What drives writing is the impulse to create a transcendent substitute for a "finitudinous" father. If this is irresponsible scholarship, Lucchesi doesn't care. In fact, it sickens him when he succumbs to following professionally acceptable conventions of scholarship: "When I cite and explain examples I become sad, even nauseous, and my syntax goes down the toilet." Instead of citing evidence for a critical point of view, he would prefer "to confuse the Myth with its autobiographical origin."

Lucchesi puts several postmodern twists on the autobiographical and psychological themes he finds in *Moby-Dick*. He rejects Ahab's quest for a "deep" truth that supposedly lies beneath the surface of sensory reality. Such a quest, he claims, relies on a "metaphysics of the sinkhole," and it can only lead to "the dull death of deep meaning." But despite that inevitable outcome, the drive to pursue metaphysical quests feels no less compelling. As an alternative, though, Lucchesi celebrates Melville's counter-impulse "to stay at the thin variegated surface of sensuous life and figurative play." Following a long-standing tradition in Melville scholarship, he associates this positive, life-affirming impulse with Ishmael. In turn, this preference for Ishmael's "'low enjoying power' of sensuous perception" brings to mind one of Lentricchia's own critical enthusiasms, Wallace Stevens, whose phrases and conceits make fleeting appearances throughout Lucchesi's narration. For example, at one point he alludes to "The Snowman" during a discussion of Chapter 102 of *Moby-Dick* ("A Bower in the Arsacides"), which he reads as an attempt to elaborate on "the nothing that is." But in contrast to Stevens and other modernist writers, Lucchesi cannot wholeheartedly accept the idea that art is superior to life.

Despite his deep interest in how art and reality interrelate, Lucchesi avoids getting lost in the tedious epistemological games that have become fashionable in a lot of recent fiction and criticism. Instead, he views writing more as will to power than representation. In the manner of Kenneth Burke (the subject of Lentricchia's *Criticism and Social Change*), Lucchesi calls attention to writing's attitudinal qualities. Although writing can function "as witness to the void," it is "an act of affirmation nevertheless, of an art rank with exfoliating vitality (the work of HM's art). The mortal yes of metaphor against the metaphysics of nihilism." In exploring Melville's use of the productive and affirmative powers of metaphor, Lucchesi supplies an almost physiological account for his fascination with obsessive analogizers like Montaigne, Robert Burton, Thomas Browne, Pierre Bayle, and William Hazlitt. An exemplary, relatively recent analog for Lucchesi's type of commentary would be William H. Gass's remarkable essay on Emerson in *Habitations of the Word* (1985).

Lucchesi's critical observations effectively characterize him as a better reader than writer. Haunted by Melville's intimidating specter, itself a major cause of his own sense of inadequacy, he can write only brief, elliptic pieces, memorable only for "a few phrases" and bearing little resemblance to the encyclopedic plenitude of "Moby HYPHEN Dick." (Among Melville scholars, it's a mark of insider status to stress the hyphen in the novel's title, as well as its absence in the whale character's name.) Instead of trying to generate his own artistic plenitude, Lucchesi finds a safer creative outlet in aesthetic appreciation. What he finds in Melville's narrative technique is the Eros-Thanatos interplay of affirming and negating moods. He considers metaphor to be primary, plot secondary. Accordingly, he believes Melville is most powerful when he lets himself succumb to the essayistic impulse, "the impulse to antistory:" "In the essay, the story-dead form of the essay; in hundreds of pages of nonfiction Melville's fluent genius finds its most imaginative form." Since a story can be told without the essay's inflections of personal style, Lucchesi claims that "Melville abandons what is best in himself" when he squanders his powers in "the pursuit of plot and character." He develops these observations by referring to an oft-cited, ominous formula from Don DeLillo's *White Noise* (1985): "All plots tend to move deathward." As in *Crimes of Art and Terror* (2003), Lentricchia's collaboration with Jody McAuliffe, this DeLillo reference suggests the close, and thoroughly ambivalent, affinity between creativity and violence. While Ahab's plot to kill the White Whale can lead only deathward, Melville's "madness of metaphor" – his "impulse to antistory" – defers death, fosters life, and fills in cosmic vacancy with human creativity. This battle of artistic and worldly impulses recalls Richard Poirier's idea that the canonical American writers found an ultimate, albeit tenuous, freedom in a "world elsewhere" of literary style. As Lucchesi puts it, "The culturally acceptable, and economically useful, impulse to write a story encounters the culturally unreadable, economically disastrous, but utterly ravishing impulse to be free of narrative death-drive."

Lentricchia inserts these meditations within a shreds-and-patches narrative that covers several stages of Lucchesi's life. The order in which he places these surrounding episodes is more or less interchangeable. But the novel's final scenes deliver a modest, if somewhat buried, climax. Throughout each episode, Melville remains a constant background presence, as when a childhood crush named Melvina, or maybe Malvina, inspires a variety of linguistic, historical, and psychological associations. For better or worse, like Melville or like Jacques Derrida, Lucchesi tends to see great significance in puns. Through elaborate punning, he links his crush on the girl to his worship of Melville, to the history of the Falkland Islands ("Islas Malvinas" is their Argentinian name), and to the act of writing as the effort to overcome both unrequited romantic love and the longing for a transcendent father.

Later in life, while teaching not only Melville but Hawthorne, Dickinson, and Whitman at a small college, Lucchesi tells his students, "I'm only here because my fiction is commercially untouchable." He turns out to be a horrible teacher because the "deep aesthetic immersion" he wants to force on his students isn't something that can be taught. He can only try to model it by staring in silence for minutes on end at a closed text, occasionally muttering, "I am all the way under. Are you?" As a result of Lucchesi's awkward failures to transmit the aesthetic habitus, the college's President decides to let him go, observing, "I don't believe that we should ever want to contain this type of person, here at Central." From a literary standpoint, the remark fits into a series of allusions to Whitman's and Melville's ability to "contain multitudes." But it also reflects present-day academia's apparent indifference to, and sometimes outright fear of, aesthetic appreciation. This is a professional development that Lentricchia has also dwelt on in *The Edge of Night* and touched on briefly in *Crimes of Art and Terror*.

By making Lucchesi's interpretations of a literary text the object of narrative development, Lentricchia follows the lead of writers like Jorge Luis Borges, Vladimir Nabokov, and Ishmael Reed. But his most important precursor is Melville's great-grandson Paul Metcalf, whose *Genoa* (1965) also focuses on *Moby-Dick* and combines fictional prose with scholarly commentary. Weaving various thematic significances into this technique, Lentricchia indulges himself with an abundance of analogies between writing and sex (not to mention the analogies between writing and excrement that James Joyce elaborates in *Finnegans Wake* with such surprising enthusiasm). For Lucchesi, the central chapter of *Moby-Dick* is "A Squeeze of the Hand" (Chapter 94), in which Ishmael finds relief from the violence and madness of Ahab's quest in "the sweet and unctuous duty" of squeezing congealed lumps of sperm back into liquid. He gets so caught up in the activity's sensual pleasures that "a strange sort of insanity" descends upon him, and he begins to squeeze his crewmen's hands and gaze sentimentally into their eyes. Commenting on this scene, Lucchesi equates the "fraternalizing force" of men working together, squeezing sperm and one another's hands, with the purpose of writing. But he also implicitly agrees with Ishmael's bittersweet insight that "man must eventually lower, or at least shift, his conceit of attainable felicity; not placing it any-where in the intellect or the fancy; but in the wife, the heart, the bed, the table, the saddle, the fire-side, the country."

Of course, either equating or opposing writ-ing with the life of the affections leads to a dilemma. On one hand, writing is Lucchesi's best means of "circulating" with others. But on the other hand, it is the very thing that cuts him off from the rest of humanity, mainly because it generates such an intense involvement with the self: "He, Thomas Lucchesi, the Scrooge of Art, who hoards himself to writing. He gives so little to others, he gives nothing, who would now reclaim his past with words." In a sequence that resonates with Hugo von Hofmannsthal's "Letter to Lord Chandos" (1902), Lucchesi displaces his regrets over self-imposed exile onto a venerable Wittgenstein scholar. Too much immersion in the solitary activities of writing and philosophizing, he claims, caused Melville, Wittgenstein, and now himself to miss out on "the greatest thing in the world: the warmth of a moist body, a kind and beautiful body. Beautiful *because* kind." But not even these regrets, nor his appreciation for Ishmael's delight in sensuous surface reality, can prevent him from returning to his role as "the mad Ahab of reading," and from repeatedly withdrawing, like Melville and Wittgenstein, into "the ice field of his mind." Since he has no family and only distant or dead friends, Lucchesi's withdrawal raises no immediate ethical complications: "With a compassion Melville never had, I never married, am childless." But his recurring surfeits of writerly solitude also make him gravitate toward domestic life, as when he formulates a genuinely moving conjecture on Melville's professional silence after publishing *The Confidence-Man* (1857). He attributes this silence to Melville's belated acknowledgment of familial obligations to his wife Elizabeth and their children. As a result, he "walked out of the ruined fortress of his love, the always already ruined fortress of his writing, where he wanted to lose his grip and dissolve in an ecstasy of composition. He came back to the actual, to the ruined

family to which, long before, he'd said no."
Readers who are familiar with Melville's biography will see nothing new in this conjecture. But it relates his life as an artist to an ethical dilemma that continues to plague the modern writer's conscience. Not only Hofmannsthal but Thomas Mann and the brilliant contemporary novelists John Banville and Richard Powers come to mind as figures who explore the solitary writer's regrets at missing out on everyday life. At the same time, though, Lentricchia joins Don DeLillo in highlighting the ethically dubious side of these regrets. The longing to affect people might reflect positive impulses of affection and solidarity. But it can also reflect a destructive desire to inflict violence and terror.

In *Lucchesi and The Whale* and *Crimes of Art and Terror*, Lentricchia places himself in the presently disfavored tradition of impressionistic, belle-lettristic criticism. In recent decades, academic criticism has drifted away from that tradition's focus on aesthetic appreciation. Instead, it tends to focus more on historical context, political subtext, and self-consuming epistemological ruminations. As a result, few academics write enthusiastically about the powers of aesthetic experience. In fact, attempts to do so can often bring on charges of elitism, naivety, and political disingenuousness. There are understandable institutional reasons for such charges, not to mention several politically legitimate reasons. But with unmistakable outrage, Lentricchia suggests that academic silence over literature's aesthetic powers stems from either trained incapacity or fear. The aesthetic powers that literature can release threaten critical conventions on several fronts: they confound theoretical classification and ideological alignment; they have dubious relations to historical causes and contexts; they can produce unforeseen social and psychological consequences; and they betray political allegiances just as readily as they serve them. For Lentricchia, it's a complex choice whether one should conform to expedient conventions and comforting obligations or immerse oneself in what Pierre Bourdieu would call the *illusio* of art. But despite his ambivalence, he puts most of his expressive enthusiasm on the side of art.

Fictions of the Self in
The Book of Ruth

JENNIFER WELLMAN

An early scene from *The Book of Ruth* should feel vaguely familiar to readers acquainted with the Modernist canon. Lentricchia here invokes none other than Joyce's *Ulysses*, in which Leopold Bloom sits "Asquat on the cuckstool" in his outhouse, reads the paper, and contemplates taking up a writing career. In Lentricchia's version, Thomas Lucchesi sits "Asquat the throne of his brooding contemplation," posing questions concerning his own status as a writer. Bloom wipes himself with a piece of the local newspaper – Joyce's sly comment on the popular press of his time. Lucchesi wipes himself, finds blood, and melodramatically concludes that he has colon cancer. Lentricchia's readers will recognize Lucchesi's short reign on his throne as a trademark of his writing. The scene further resonates with the literary past and our own times. The humor is self-referential and self-deprecating – the blood on the paper is described as "Frank, and more than a little." It is also a moment of what Lentricchia describes elsewhere as "terrific comedy," a uniquely American mode that mixes humor with our deepest fears and anxieties. The anxiety expressed here concerns the state of contemporary literature and the state of the dying (or as postmodernists would insist, already dead) author. This anxiety underlies much of the plot in *The Book of Ruth*. What is the place and function of literature in a world dominated by media-created images, and in which art is treated as one more commodity in the marketplace? What, moreover, is the role of the writer in a culture that has proclaimed "the death of the author?"

In *The Book of Ruth*, Lentricchia addresses these questions in his portrayal of Lucchesi, the anxious novelist. Alienated by contemporary media, politics and consumerism, Lucchesi believes his body of work to be a failure, and despairs of ever creating anything great. But Lucchesi is more than a mere character; he is a concept. "The idea of Lucchesi," as Lentricchia calls it, dramatically shapes the narrative structure of the novel. Lentricchia creates both the character of the author, and he fashions a characteristic narrative for him. Lucchesi's voice pervades *The Book of Ruth*, speaking in both the first and third person. It is, in effect, a voice of self creation, and attempts to build a coherent self-vision from the evocation of other literary and popular narratives. At the same time, *The Book of Ruth* calls into question these narratives. Through the juxtaposition of narratives, Lentricchia criticizes the use and abuse of art in contemporary culture, while also demonstrating its necessity.

At once a tragic and comic character, Lucchesi is a fragmented man who attempts to piece together a coherent understanding of himself and the world out of the various cultural narratives available to him. He is described as having "no faith: not in Ruth, not in himself, not in his art, not in God." Living in the absence of these stabilizing truths, Lucchesi suffers from what he calls, quoting Pope, "this long disease, my life." Described by his wife Ruth as her "man of changes," Lucchesi inhabits a number of different personae throughout the novel: tortured artist, obsessive hypochondriac, jealous husband, and self-mocking clown. Ruth photographs Lucchesi's many changes, and he gives the impression of watching himself from the outside. Lucchesi often interprets and defines his life through literature. Mourning his lack of status as a writer, Lucchesi paraphrases Emily Dickinson: "My life stands a loaded gun;" and when Lucchesi and Ruth are invited by their Iraqi guide, Mahmood, to visit Magdi al-Radi,

Lucchesi comments to Ruth that he is sure they're characters in an espionage novel he once read.

The Book of Ruth is rife with such literary allusions: Ruth and Lucchesi retreat to their Walden-like refuge in the Adirondacks, all described with references to the Transcendentalists. Lentricchia later refers to Hart Crane's "The Bridge." But the most important work Lentricchia engages is Eliot's "The Waste Land," which Ruth paraphrases: "Speak to me. Speak. Can you not speak?" Her response to Lucchesi's habit of bedtime poetic quotations challenges his self-definition. He is not a poet of untapped potential; he is unable to act because, like Eliot's weary modern man (and his poem), Lucchesi is a collection of fragments.

Lucchesi's search for a cure for his malaise runs throughout the novel, with its many shifts in perspective. At one point, Ruth speaks of herself and the physical and sexual comfort she has to offer Lucchesi as a sort of remedy. Trying to assuage Lucchesi's insecurities at bedtime, Ruth tells him, "I know a miracle cure for your literary tongue. Would you like to take the cure now?" In her letter to Ruth, the ambitious editor Lois Gint describes herself as a "cure" for both Lucchesi and Ruth since she offers fame and critical acclaim as a panacea for two disillusioned and neglected artists. Another possible remedy or escape for Lucchesi is in his creative activity. Throughout the novel, we are given the impression that he is narrating his own story. From the beginning, he conveys the impression of a man split in two by his own self-consciousness. Terrified by the inevitability of death, he seeks wholeness in a fictional creation of himself. He first appears looking in a mirror and, confronted with his image, he expresses anxiety over the aged, deteriorating face he sees. Doubling this visual image, the language on the page mirrors the split between self and self-as-other that Lucchesi experiences: "Lucchesi mourns for Lucchesi." Lucchesi-the-subject mourns for Lucchesi-the-object-of-pity. Claiming that there can be "no joy, no intimacy, no refuge, nothing at all . . . except in the art of his fiction," Lucchesi invents a fictional "Junior" for himself. Even though this suffix is not on his birth certificate, he nonetheless scrawls the word lovingly after his name since it creates for him an illusory younger self.

The idea of "Junior" not only grants Lucchesi the illusion of youth, it also enables him to think of himself in the third person. In his article on Don DeLillo ("*Libra* as Postmodern Critique") Lentricchia discusses the characteristically American impulse to self-create – to exchange the flawed first person "I" for an idealized third person construction. For Lucchesi, the name "Junior" represents an idealized version of himself in the same way that Jay Gatsby – to use Lentricchia's example – embodies the desired ideal of James Gatz in *The Great Gatsby*. The actual name "Junior" is mentioned only in the first scene of *The Book of Ruth*, but the echoes of Lucchesi's idealized version of himself resound throughout the novel. This youthful version resurfaces in the form of a farce that gestures towards its fictional construction. At seventy-one, Lucchesi is described as "a v-shaped specimen of manhood still [. . .] with well-toned pectorals, [which] had not yet yielded to gravity, would apparently never yield." The narrating voice of Lucchesi undercuts this romantic notion of Lucchesi through humor and exaggeration.

Lucchesi also seeks to define himself through various narratives taken from the culture at large, creating his own story as a kind of pastiche of American cultural history. The central component of Lucchesi's narrativized self-concept is his "myth" of his wife, against whom he defines himself. He creates a myth of Ruth that is at once idealized and unattainable, much like Gatsby's vision of Daisy. And Lucchesi perpetuates this ideal throughout the novel. His version of Ruth draws on a number of sources, though

it's largely based on the legend the media created about her much-reprinted book, *Cuban
Stories*. Upon her return to the United States
from a visit to Cuba during the 1960s, Ruth
Cohen, a twenty-one-year-old college student,
became a pop phenomenon – "the scarlet photographer" one newspaper dubbed her. Art critics raved that she had perfectly captured "the
emergence of the postmodern body, self-stylized
and trapped in perpetual political theater." Her
art was praised for being in tune with the times,
and for setting "an impossible standard in the art
of artlessness." Interpreters considered her work
free of emotion and self-referentiality; her subjects appeared unfiltered by the photographer's
presence. In this way, Ruth's pictures became a
paradigm of a postmodern aesthetic: images that
posit no author or origin upon which to fix
meaning.

The critical acclaim for *Cuban Stories* is only
part of Ruth's legend. While critics praised
Ruth's work for its lack of reference to her presence as photographer, the popular media became obsessed with her personal life, or, to be
more specific, with the narrative it created of her
personal life, based in part on rumors that she
slept with both Castro and JFK. She becomes a
media icon, documented in Walter Winchell's
column and a memoir by Gore Vidal; more a

cult figure than an artist. The savvy editor Lois
Gint wants Ruth to go to Iraq because she
guesses – correctly it turns out – that Saddam
will be aware of Ruth's legend and will submit
to her camera.

Lucchesi embraces the media evaluation of
Ruth's work not just because it it great art, but
because it has political significance. He laments
the absence of politics in his own work: he com-
plains to Ruth during a morning walk, "My fiction is irrelevant. Everyone knows this." Lucchesi
longs to achieve the political importance of Ruth's
work, but in the process he alienates himself from
Ruth herself. When he becomes obsessed with
coverage of the first Gulf War, Lucchesi glues
himself to the television and ignores his wife, who
moves into an apartment across the street. When
she protests that his infatuation is unhealthy,
Lucchesi responds, "Iraq is my Cuba . . . A fair-
minded person would understand – would be
sympathetic. Would want me to have my day as
she had her day. I think of it as a day for art."
Lucchesi's idealization of Ruth and her art shapes
his self-perception; it also separates him physically from her.

The stories concerning Ruth's alleged sexual
exploits also make Lucchesi feel inadequate and
jealous. He cannot escape the idea that men are
sexually attracted to her and that she may

respond to their advances. In this regard, Lucchesi demonstrates a kind of double awareness, as he recognizes that these mediated narratives are false, yet he allows them to influence his relationship. Even after Lucchesi has apparently accepted Ruth's versions of her brief acquaintances with Castro and JFK – meetings which involved no sex – he still worries that her meeting with Saddam might have some sexual consequences.

Lucchesi constantly incorporates these misleading narratives into his own myth of Ruth. As Lentricchia writes at the beginning of the novel, "He can't help himself, it's an addiction, this persistent mythifying of her." The myth of Ruth is also Lucchesi's vision of an actual woman who holds the cure for what ails him: "Ruth is real." And Ruth's realness represents a wholeness that Lucchesi, whose consciousness is divided between self and representation of self, cannot achieve. She is not, like him, plagued by the "murderous mirror." She is, in fact, uninterested in her appearance; she does not look in mirrors; her picture does not appear on the jacket of *Cuban Stories*. The physical presence of Ruth forms a contrast with Lucchesi's linguistic obsession – she offers the pleasures of her body as a cure for his literary logorrhea. Ruth would rather make love than talk, and on numerous occasions Lucchesi's obsessive need to discuss politics or Ruth's past drives her away from the bed. His belief that she somehow remains his cure is echoed by the local poet laureate who dubs her "The Lady of Ninth Lake" – a name that alludes to Arthurian legend and the woman who rescues Lancelot as a child and cures him when he is mad. It also invokes Ruth's association with "Those famous men of Camelot," the coterie surrounding JFK, who Lucchesi calls "King Arthur."

While the voice of Lucchesi is engaged in enunciating this myth of Ruth, the novel itself offers a critique of both the myth and its sources, whether it's Ruth as romantic heroine or sultry spy. The actual story that Ruth tells about Cuba turns out to be neither a typical espionage thriller nor a romance, though aspects of both play a role. Her tale of what really happened in Cuba provides what Don DeLillo calls in his essay, "In the Ruins of the Future," a "counter-narrative:" a story that confronts the accepted version of history and offers a different reading of events. From Ruth's perspective, the trip to Cuba is not about adventure, love, or even the birth of her art; it is about the violent deaths of three people and her inability to prevent them. Ruth's self-understanding is far from the media's image of an adventurous American girl who boldly partakes in the politics of her time by representing the real conditions in Cuba. Duped and manipulated by her own government, Ruth recalls how her interrogator tells her before she witnesses the execution of the Cubans: "You are an American fool. You know nothing . . . I am going to give you a Cuban memory." In Ruth's counter-narrative, the pictures she brings home do not, as critics claim, represent the true story of Cuba during the Missile Crisis. The real story of her time in Cuba is burnished in her memory: the faces of those in whose deaths she is implicated.

Ruth's telling of the Kennedy encounter provides another counter-narrative. Instead of a sexy story of power and intrigue, Ruth narrates what Lucchesi disparages as "domestic realism." JFK, suffering from Addison's disease, looks jaundiced, and Jackie is pale and emotionally scarred from the recent death of her two-day-old son. All of this is far less glamorous than the standard Camelot tale, and Lentricchia takes it a step further with his sense of humor and parody. When Kennedy and Ruth discuss the government's manipulation of her in Cuba, John Jr. smears both JFK and Ruth with ketchup. The President remarks, "The literary types would call this a symbolic moment, but I am not particularly literary, Miss Cohen. Let's not tell Gore Vidal." Such a scene pokes fun at the way literary types over-read meaning into texts. It also mocks the truth claims of a powerful memoirist such as Vidal. As Lois Gint claims in her letter to Ruth: "Gore was there. Gore *knows*. Even when Gore's not there, Gore knows." Regardless of what actually happened at the barbecue, the story that Vidal and others tell becomes truth by virtue of its being told well.

Lentricchia further debunks the myth of Ruth through the language he attributes to critical reviews of her art, which misinterpret and misappropriate her work. Critics initially praised and embraced her photos; with a "pontificating sentence about her 'noble reticence,'" one critic assured her position in the ranks of great American photographers. Strong stuff for a young woman who had taken only one photography class at Sarah Lawrence. Later critics are even more off base, now dismissing Ruth's book as passe: "Hers is the wilted salad of yesterday's avant-garde." Such wildly disparate reviews undercut the authority of arts criticism itself – a doubt shared by the self-confessed former critic Lentricchia.

Lentricchia similarly mocks mainstream journalism with its language of violent and abusive love. At one point, reporters "pummel" Ruth with questions; later, she and Lucchesi are "assaulted" by a radio pundit's blather. At the most extreme is the trendy magazine editor Gint with her language of rape – she wants to "ram this assignment so hard up Cohen's ass she'll squeal for more." Though her tone in her letters is mostly violent and sexual, she opens with the tired language from the much-quoted sonnet by Elizabeth Barrett Browning, "How do I love? Let me count the ways." Gint's brutal description of anal rape certainly undermines her hyperbolic proclamation of love.

Gint's characterization of her profession as a "devouring lover" connects to the notion of ghouls that runs throughout the novel. As Lucchesi explains, the word itself comes from an Arabic word meaning "to seize and to eat." Ruth, though, associates ghouls with those who feed upon people and their histories for personal pleasure or profit. When Lucchesi protests Ruth's use of the word, thinking that she really means ghosts, she corrects him: "There are ghosts who are ghouls. They feed on the living." Such was the media frenzy that greeted her first and only book, and it happens again when Lucchesi disappears in Iraq. In Ruth's view, *New Yorker* editor Gint and the publisher of Knopf are two of the "chief ghouls;" and both are thrilled with Lucchesi's disappearance since they know it will mean big sales for the magazine and for reprints of Lucchesi's otherwise forgotten novels.

Lucchesi himself is a bit of a ghoul in his quest to achieve fame and critical acclaim. Early in his relationship with Ruth, he dreams that the woman he loves will also help him achieve recognition. He proposes one such fantasy during one of their morning walks: "Photos by Cohen, text by Lucchesi. Your long anticipated second book appears at last in collaboration with the long-anticipated lover. The obscure writer carried at last into the light by the reluctant and once famous photographer." Furthermore, he has fed upon Ruth's art and her history, and he knows it. In a conversation with Ruth about ghouls, he warns himself that one way to resist becoming one is to "Refuse to act upon the person of another . . . Want as little as possible. Stop the monologues." But he cannot resist his ghoulish impulses.

The cure Lucchesi seeks, not surprisingly, lies outside himself. The trip to Iraq provides Lucchesi with the ultimate counter-narrative; in Baghdad, he is an outsider – he doesn't understand the language and people avoid him because he's American. Mahmood tells him about the sufferings Iraq experienced after the first Gulf War, the war Lucchesi watched on TV with such eager – one might say ghoulish – relish. Mahmood's stories also provide another counter-narrative to the televised American version of events. Moreover, in the strange museum of Magda al-Radi, Lucchesi and Ruth study the material products of America on display: a vintage typewriter, a washing machine, cigarettes, jujubes, a copy of *The Great Gatsby*, a bottle of Coke, hair tonic. The true representation of America, Magda claims, pointing to her collection. "We are all Americans now. Stupid to resist." Lucchesi counters that it is not the physical things that represent America, but the idea we have of these things. Pointing to his head, he states, "It's in here. It's better in here . . . What's in a name? If we have the name, we don't need the thing because we already have the thing. Everything is in a name." Lucchesi testifies to the power of words and narrative to shape both individuals and an entire culture.

Throughout *The Book of Ruth*, the voice of Lucchesi demonstrates how competing narratives of our culture shape our identity. But Lentricchia doesn't leave us hopeless. He recognizes that our lives are built upon narratives and that we can choose which narratives we will make our own. At the end of the novel, Ruth explains to Lucchesi's doctor, Larry Shapiro, that she allows her Russian tenants to plant cherry trees in her backyard because she believes that they are planting memories. As Ruth explains, "The fruit of a good memory is good living. A good memory has to be cultivated alongside the bad ones, which we assiduously cultivate, because it's hard not to . . . Because the good ones nourish the living in their struggle against the ghouls, who prefer that we dwell on the bad ones." Ruth recognizes the ability to choose her own narrative which is exactly what she does at the end of her story. She assumes the name and appearance of a local Italian woman and wears a Russian scarf in the style of an Iraqi. In the absence of Lucchesi, the previous author of her everyday myth, Ruth re-creates herself.

The Book of Ruth argues for the value of literature in contemporary culture and serves as its own evidence. In a world debased by pop imagery and commodified art, we do not have to accept the dominant narratives imposed upon us. Literature provides us with the knowledge and power to expose these narratives for what they are. It frees us to create a self and, though the ghouls remain in the world, we resist becoming ghouls ourselves.

"Where they are supposed to get you right"

Utica and Lentricchia's "New Modernistic" Regionalism

NICHOLAS BIRNS

When the well-respected critic Frank Lentricchia (born 1940) began to shift his energies from criticism to fiction in the 1990s, reviewers noted the works' experimental technique and their autobiographical context, particularly their tendency to be set in or with reference to the upstate New York city of Utica, where Lentricchia grew up and went to college. But the discussions of Lentricchia's work have tended to passively accept the Utica setting rather than actively articulate it. This essay seeks to foreground not only the particularities of the Utica setting but how it operates as an interpretive and framing element in Lentricchia's oeuvre, which now extends over several novels: the diptych *Johnny Critelli* and *The Knifemen* (1996), *The Music of the Inferno* (1999), *Lucchesi And The Whale* (2001), and the most recent, *The Book of Ruth* (2005).

Lentricchia's Utica encompasses both the city's slim connection to the Founding Fathers and its current status as a community largely inhabited by Italian Americans and other white ethnics and in long-term, post-industrial economic crisis. There is both continuity and discontinuity between Anglo and Italian inaugurators. Historicity, but a modernist historicity; a postmodern version in the normative sense would make this a magical-realist panoply, a reaffirmation of the saving irrationality and messiness of history itself; but for Lentricchia, the messiness, though there, is certainly not saving. Lentricchia's Utica is a swaggering, macho world, like the Old West or Melville's whaling-boats. The Utica Meat episode in *The Knifemen* depicts initiation into male adulthood as a scene of bloody contestation in which all achievement is reduced to the survival of the strongest, or at least the one who can endure the most pummeling. But, interestingly, it is the women associated with the Utica milieu who seem to have manifested the greatest worldly accomplishment – for example, an "attending physician" who "is one of the few women at that time in the Upstate Medical Center. She stepped out of Botticelli. Taciturn, intense, mythic." And the most surprising character of all in Lentricchia's Utica saga is Ruth Cohen. "Ruth" and "Utica" sound alike; yet Ruth supplies the great dimension of what is outside Utica in Lentricchia's fictional oeuvre. Photojournalist to the world, confidant of Fidel Castro and the late Saddam Hussein, the aura of internationalism and cosmopolitan success previously personified in the Lentricchia fictional oeuvre only by the ghost of Herman Melville is epitomized by Ruth. Ruth nonetheless periodically gravitates back to Lucchesi and to Utica, to care for them, to salvage them, to acknowledge them. That it is the man who stays home, rooted in the region, that he is Penelope to Ruth's Odysseus, is one of the striking permutations and reversals in the Lentricchia oeuvre.

And the revelation of Ruth also changes how the Utica region itself is depicted. There is an extension eastward, towards the Adirondacks reaching out into the country, not confined or immured in merely urban circumstances. In *Ruth*, a hinterland is revealed: Utica's Adirondacks. The Adirondacks to which Utica is "gateway" are not New York City's Adirondacks, a place of luxury rustic retreat, but a hardscrabble land of "flowers, ferns, lichens and mosses." Not the rough-hewn sublime of the later nineteenth century (the earlier nineteenth century could not "see" the Adirondacks as the latter part did; James Fenimore Cooper wrote about them without seeming to register what others later saw as their beauty and wildness). But this is low-scale, cubist, modernist, western slope Adirondack landscape: "Partridgeberry, sheep laurel, trout lilies, fiddlehead ferns, crustose lichens and caribou moss. The names of things are lies. There are no caribou in the Adirondacks. Never were. The earth is 4.6 billion years old. Where were they all then, the partridgeberry, the sheep laurel, the fiddlehead ferns?" Lentricchia puts the Adirondacks under the auspices of geology, not botany or biology; a modernist science dealing with the made thing, the shaped, but not the infused product; carving, not modeling. Names are lies; Ninth Lake is applied to a certain lake that is not designated as such on the map, but is Ruth's ultimate vector of retreat; a kind of quintessence plus four, an image of what is just outside of boundaries. Ninth Lake, Boonville at the junction of those two endlessly gray, roving roads of northern New York state, 12 and 28, are places, have a density to them, but they also possess an abstraction, a sense of being site as well as locale, a stage as much as a context.

The wider scope revealed in *Ruth* focuses Lentricchia's persistent reader and just what Utica and its region has meant to the author: both a lived and intensely felt place that the reader is meant to link to the author's biographical experience, and a conjured, imagined field of meaning.

"Utica" as a referent, whether in Africa or in America, always denoted a second city. Utica in North Africa was the earlier Phoenician settlement, but Carthage, its later sister city, far outstripped it in glory. Utica, though, escaped Carthage's brutal sack by the Romans, still sputtering on after Carthage burned. Given that Rome and Carthage fought many of their battles over Sicily, and that Lentricchia's fictional alter egos are of partially Sicilian background, it is fitting that the community of Italian-Americans living in East Utica and depicted in the Lentricchia oeuvre settled in a place whose name would not have been unfamiliar to their ancestors.

Lentricchia is not silent in his oeuvre about the link between the Italian and the African. In *The Music of the Inferno,* Robert Tagliaferro's Uncle Morris says: "My grandmother came over from the southern side of Sicily, where they had a considerable amount of warm interaction with the people of Africa." The surname Taliaferro – spelled this way, a family name, originally Italian, which became naturalized in the American South due to the seventeenth-century emigration of a family of that name, generates a referential tie between Italy and African Americans and whites of British descent. Former Speaker of the House Samuel Taliaferro Rayburn and Booker Taliaferro Washington indeed, as Uncle Morris points out, shared this middle name (a coincidence worthy of a Ralph Ellison novel). "Taliaferro" conveys a sense of the Italian-American bridging, in a Mediterranean way, racial and continental differences. (That the name was often pronounced "Toliver" adds another layer of irony to this fascinating story).

So multiethnicity is both in back and in front of Lentricchia's Italian-American characters. It is the *place* where these tropes of ethnicity are ventilated though that is all-important. The North American Utica is also a second or, in its state context, even fifth or sixth or thirteenth city; second in its region certainly to Syracuse, to Rochester, with its heritage of corporate abundance and even Rome, whose association with the 10th Mountain Division have kept it afloat economically, given that the military is seldom in recession. One might go to Rome and Syracuse, larger in the New World as they were in the Old, on business; Utica, in Lentricchia's oeuvre, is depicted as a place where people either hurriedly leave or stolidly stay. People leave Utica for good, are described as "recently out of Utica." The Princeton-educated mayor in *The Knifemen* asks for "Italian gaiety," pigeonholing place and ethnicity, seeing it as a conveniently accessible other, stashed in a provincial and discernible box.

Lentricchia, though, does not just write about Utica as such, but a specific Italian-American community in East Utica, centered on Mary Street: a place at once organic, teeming with raw life, but also stabbed by decay, despair, disillusion, and dysfunctionality: immured by them, but still constituting a world worth observing, worth excavating. "[T]he north, or poorer side of Mary Street, side of narrow two-family homes, then cross, at the appropriate point, to the south side of much better kept two- and three-family structures, with porches on all floors sweeping along importantly across the entire front face." Mary and Bleecker streets, as the map in *The Music of the Inferno* indicates, both run east west from Mohawk, Mary separated from Bleecker by Elizabeth; the point is that the same layout is found on actual topographical maps. Lentricchia's Utica is not a "Yoknapatawpha"; it may not always refer to real people in the literal sense but the places are real. The name Mary Street (an unusual one in the U.S.A.) evokes a pervasive Catholicism along with a sense of some sort of truncation or brokenness in the efficacy of this faith, represented by the mere fact of geographical fixity. So it is not the physical location of Utica that contests its full access to the national center, to the American colossus. It is its psychic, ethnic, and interior location.

What is "New Modernistic" rather than postmodern is this insistence on interiority, even though Lentricchia is far more pessimistic about interiority than Woolf, Joyce, or Proust, though perhaps of a similar temperament in this respect to Faulkner. The New Modernistic restaurant in the text is a kind of joke – despite the revamped name, the cuisine and ambience are no better than the old one, without the reassuring quality of having been the venue of the protagonist's childhood, but it still does indicate a persistence to contend with the questions of modernity rather than subsume them in a postmodern free-for-all of either total cacophony or passive acceptance of the given.

There is a difference between portraying an Italian American community in Utica and in New York or Las Vegas or Los Angeles. In this way, to bring in the two most famous mass media depictions of Italian Americans, Lentricchia's fictional universe has more in common with what Lance Strate calls (in his essay in *This Thing of Ours,* 2002) the north Jersey "media ecology" of the Sopranos than the Little Italy of Mario Puzo's New York-set novels and the famous movies based on them. There is a sense of being in the provinces and of the characters feeling the extra stresses, the additional impingements, of the provincial location; to be a Mafioso or just a local neighborhood denizen in the big town is different than being such in the Jersey suburbs or in Utica. To be subordinated in the provinces, as any number of students of nineteenth century fiction from Lukács to Moretti would agree, is different than to be a proletarian in the metropolis.

In Lentricchia's adulthood, Italian Americans have become swing voters, as numerous sociologists have noted. But at the same time that occurred, there was a certain circumscribing and stereotyping of Italian American ethnicity, as signified by *The Godfather* movies and other pop-culture stereotypes. The place of Lentricchia's Utica in the ontological landscape of late modernity has to do with both the trauma of past violence and discrimintion and the sense that communities like Utica do not have access to the wider world the way they should in a fully democratic and transparent society. Just as Lucchesi needs Ruth Cohen's star power to give him access to *The New Yorker*, just as her global reach galvanizes his local vulnerability into action, Utica seems indurated, lost, an object of mourning, separated and annealed from the wider world. Yet the community Lentricchia depicts was never pre-modern in the sense of being an unsullied, organic *Gemienschaft*. The fact that the quintessential East Utica restaurant is called the Modernistic points to how the twentieth century, in all its multiplicity, was the locale for this community's aspirations and setbacks. Lentricchia displays the woundedness of modernism, its resistance to euphoric end-of-history certainties.

Just as the Modernistic restaurant is renamed the New Modernistic with little outward but some inner displacement, Upstate New York takes on a different representation once it has been perceived as being in decline and crisis. For all the suffering, elegy, and lamentation, there is an opportunity to be seized at the breaking of consensus. Utica is that which it has been told it is: irrelevant to postmodernity. In fact the term "Rust Belt" basically means that part of modernity which has been told is irrelevant to "postmodernity." While some cities have done just fine in the postmodern era like New York or Los Angeles.

Lucchesi and The Whale sets up a dramatic antinomy between the colossus of the American literary tradition, Herman Melville, and Lucchesi, a modern-day, experimental writer conscious of the magnitude and breadth of

American literary tradition but also aware of his sufferings, and the collective sufferings of his ancestors. Lucchesi's identity is unstable to the extent people never get his name right:

> Makes a phonetic list in his notebook of the mispronunciations that he's heard of his surname in America: Luck-easy, Lou-seize-ee, Lou-chee-zee; Lou-keys-ee (one of his cousins!); Lou-cheese-eye; Lou-keys-eye; Lou-casy (one of his uncles!), Lou-kay-zee (*yes!*)

As often occurs, sports fans have an advantage in these cross-cultural matters, as Frank Lucchesi, the manager of the Texas Rangers during the 1970s, always had his name pronounced correctly by sportscasters who presumably got it from the horse's mouth. (In a coincidence that addresses preoccupations of Lentricchia's critical oeuvre, one of the players Lucchesi managed was a relief pitcher named Steve Foucault.)

Lentricchia, of course, is "really" talking about his own surname, and its ramifications. In 1985, I was asked by a fellow student at Columbia University to recommend an introductory book on deconstruction and contemporary criticism. I recommended Lentricchia's *After the New Criticism*. The classmate, who herself had an Italian surname, was perplexed at the name "Lentricchia": clearly, it did not seem like the name of a European cultural authority; it seemed too "close to home"; it was in this way a more markedly American name than the most Anglo of surnames in this circumstance could have been.

"Lucchesi" and "Lentricchia," though, are not in totally complementary distribution. The name of Lentricchia is actually mentioned in the fictional oeuvre. People named Lentricchia are side-presences; the protagonists of the works are never named Lentricchia, but the name is not entirely absent; a Lucchesi-universe does not exclude the presence of Lentricchias. This grain-iness of separation between fact and fiction is the scrabbly attribute of Lentricchia's focal scrutiny. Lucchesi in some ways resembles John Updike's Rabbit, a version of Updike who never left eastern Pennsylvania, or Philip Roth's various protagonists who are versions of himself who never left northern New Jersey. What is different is that the real writer is not totally kept out of the internal fiction, as in Updike, or introduced in a flagrantly metafictive way, as in Roth. It is part of the letter of the fictional fabric. The writer's subjectivity hovers over, but never suffocates, the material. The fact that, in verbal or sentential terms, the subject is missing in so many of Lentricchia's sentences, lends a sense of Hemingway in its sparseness. It also leads to a paradoxical heightening of the subjectivity behind the missing verbal subject – a referent just off the map.

And Lucchesi sees this subjectivity not only in himself (and, inferentially, his creator), but also in that of the author of "The Whale," Herman Melville himself. It is interesting in this respect that Melville's great family triumph before his own generation, which scholars such as the late Michael Paul Rogin (in *Subversive Genealogy*, 1983) have seen as integral to his psychological makeup, was the role of his grandfather, Peter Gansevoort, who was the hero of the 1777 battle of Fort Stanwix, near Utica. Melville, though, made himself larger, transcended America, told America by telling it slant, at sea; in terms of cultural status, he became the whale he wrote about. Lucchesi is doggedly, stubbornly, local, of his own place even when he is not in it.

Home, Lucchesi once muses, is "where they are supposed to know you" but they mostly do not: they know him as a child, know his role in their families, but have little sense of his adult psyche, his adult intelligence, his adult sufferings. Yet Lucchesi is willing to let himself be defined by the place, have its weaknesses and sufferings be his own. There is vulnerability, even mortification, in this; but this is all the organic connection there is. There is not a Romantic continuity of self and community; it manifests itself in an abstract, jagged, cubistic or 'modernistic' way. Yet there is one referent in *Lucchesi and The Whale* which shows how fungible both local and global reference can be. When the Falklands War between Britain and Argentina breaks out in 1982, Lucchesi is reminded, by the Argentine name for the islands, "Las Malvinas," of a girl named Malvina he knew in elementary school. This leads to a wild, extraordinarily inventive riff on the name "Malvinas," which originally was given by the French in honor of St. Malo:

> Lucchesi decides to express himself. Writes: These islands are small. "Saint" in old French is figurative for "inner sanctum." The Falklands, the inner sanctum of small evils? So I compose; so I would compose myself on my small island, this writing room.
> Like Lucchesi, the Malvinas are not arable, they are treeless, and monotonously bleak, except for the millions of penguins which journey up from the neighboring ice world of Antarctica to mate. [*Cold Copulars*] Mean temperature: 42 Fahrenheit, with winds constant from all directions at twenty miles per hour, periodically sustained at gale force. Lucchesi thinks about the wind chill factor. Lucchesi feels no chill.

Even though the Falkland Islands were mentioned by Melville, at least once in *Redburn*, they are, in psycho-topographical terms, closer to

Lucchesi than the Whale: overlooked, distant, a frigid sanctuary. And, again, there is not just a geographical but psychological resonance; there is an innerness here: Lentricchia is not content for the self to simply be a determinant or epiphenomenon of place. To use a phrase from Lentricchia's critical work, it is not Utica *an sich*, but "someone reading" Utica, and this splaying of inner self and region, this sense of a mental landscape existing even in the descent of the northern modern, is redolent of twentieth-century abstraction. Lentricchia, aside from his theoretical work, has specialized, in his academic career, in modern poetry, and of all the people he has written about the closest to his own rationalistic vision is Wallace Stevens. Indeed, Lucchesi identifies himself as a "Wallace Stevens of this neighborhood." One thinks particularly of some of Stevens' brief late lyrics, in which places are named, lovingly, evocatively but never conclusively.

The region, as an indexical reference, is at once a minute register of particularity, and an inessential coloring of an abstract condition. It is Modernist regionalism. The regionalism of Stevens, William Carlos Williams, Faulkner, and even lesser figures like Glenway Wescott is not like the local color regionalism of the nineteenth century – Lucchesi laughingly compares himself to Rose Terry Cooke and, more locally, he might have mentioned Marietta Holley. There is, in Lentricchia, no emphasis on the people and folkways of the region, but a sense of the region as achieved metaphor for limitation and, in a Joycean sense, paralysis. Regionalism in modernity became a thing. Although one does learn a lot about Utica history, both Anglo and Italian, it is made clear that this content, although interesting and not without significance to the author, is not the point. Ideas of place can be applied to phenomena outside of place as strictly defined. The rugged, fractured not necessarily empirically describable actuality of life. The body itself, as seen in Lucchesi's colon cancer in *Ruth*, becomes a site. Even the frequent references to specific sexual processes in the books are not libidinal, but corporeal, and underscore the proximity of the body to place. What Bill Brown calls "object matter" (in *A Sense of Things*, 2003) encompasses, in Lentricchia's case, both place and body. Postmodernist regionalism would largely suggest American (Latin American-influenced) magic realism, but modernist regionalism is both real and fictive, adamant on keeping those shadings distinct and revealing them to the reader through para-geological layering. Lentricchia is not modernist because he is belated, or because he has made modernism his particular field of academic study. His regionalism is modernist because this latest of modernisms is a way for the writer to keep faith with his background, and people, and his aesthetic vision, all at once. In fashioning his own Utica, Lentricchia provides least of all a place where people get you right; nor is he necessarily out to get Utica right. His surprising and jagged abstraction, though, reveals a moving tableau of a place with respect to which Lentricchia is simultaneously an escapee, an elegist, and a fierce advocate.

The Trick's Sick Songs

ANDREW DUBOIS

Frank has it out for Bing. Or does he have it out for Frank?

In *The Book of Ruth* the reader discovers Saddam Hussein listening to Sinatra in his terminal spider hole. Saddam also plays Sinatra in the midst of attempted seduction. His right hand man Habib says, "'Saddam loves Frank Sinatra.' Saddam replies and Habib says, 'But not Bing Crosby. Nix on *der Bingle*!'" With fans like that, who needs enemies.

In *The Knifemen* Frank puts forward the sick and malicious theory, the depraved conjecture that Bing Crosby was tied up in the death of Russ Columbo. You probably know all about it. Popular early crooner, circumstance of death is odd to say the least. Antique pistol. Guy didn't know it was loaded. Just happened to have a match. Sets it off. Unexpected blast. Columbo killed by ricochet. Bullet to the brain. Bing behind it. Truth buried. Shady world we live in.

Perhaps there is some plausibility to it. Frank claims he was making it up. Yet I refer you to a review of *A Prisoner of Love*, a biography of Columbo, appearing in issue 143 (summer 2006) of *Bing*, the official magazine of the International Crosby Circle, the world's oldest extant fan club, where it is said that the author of *A Prisoner of Love* "is at his best in reconstructing the death scene and the police investigation and inquest that followed [Columbo's death] and at his worst suggesting it may have been the result of a plot master-minded by Everett Crosby to eliminate competition." Everett of course was Bing's brother and business manager.

Now Bing recorded an album on Decca called *Some Old Chestnuts*, which may personally be my favorite album by Bing. It's hard to say. There are some good ones as well as some stinkers, relatively speaking. Usually pretty solid all around. The "Honeysuckle Rose" on *Some Old Chestnuts* is especially superb....The point here being that this made-up theory of Frank's is apparently also an old chestnut roasted in the rumor mill of that storied sub-sub-discipline, Russ Columbo Studies.

You can't make this stuff up, even when you make it up. It's written up, like, conjured up.

Come to think of it, whether it matters or not is hard to say, but it's not actually Frank who advances the Columbo-Crosby theory in *The Knifemen*, but a guy named Victor who's a back-alley abortionist, although he doesn't really do abortions in an alley. This so-called "character" Victor speculates on this particular sick twist of the history of popular song while gathering his things in preparation to operate on the mayor of Utica's daughter. This Victor, who incidentally "croons" on several occasions, says, "'Crosby stinks.'" He says, "'Crosby is taking it up the ass.'"

So I got to ask myself what kinds of aspersions are these, cast not only upon a fine example of the Irish people, Bing Crosby, but cast also upon the fine people of Sinatra, Columbo, Lentricchia, not to mention Jerry Vale, insofar as these words just had to be put in the mouth of a sick, sick man, this Victor. Who could stomach such aspersions? What sickness could cause their having been puked forth? Such talk from the mouths of such men as Victor and Saddam is about as vile as the once common gossip that the JFK assassination was payback against the Irish for the earlier orchestration by the Irish of the accidental death of Columbo, an angle on that day in Dallas that, one must admit, no matter what one's ethnic predilections or propensity for slander, has been woefully and no doubt deliberately avoided of late. Maybe better to let sleeping dogs lie. Victor says, "'I remember Crosby. I'm saying the voice of Russ Columbo could not

122

be resisted.'" He says, "'Russ Columbo poured it in while you slept. You woke up with the voice in your body.'" One of these quotes alludes to a Jerry Vale album and the other to a Shakespeare play. That is what we're dealing with here. We're dealing with that kind of person.

Of the many things I value about Frank's fiction, the thing I value most is how it sounds. I value the portrait of Utica, growing like a reef, a history, and the constant consideration of human things like what it means to be born, to be born *to* someone, to a family, to this particular family, these people, to leave or be orphaned, to orphan oneself. What it means to be dark, make something, man, to write, relationships new, renewed, and frayed, to try out love, somebody, to age, approach death, to die, of late. I value the choice words poached from other writers, the methods redeployed. I value the meditations on art. The medicated artist. I value the melancholy, the hypochondria, and the gouts of rage, the fact that it is funny. The O.E.D. The dialogue. The monologue. Variety of voice and genre. But most of all I value how it sounds.

Oh! Shades immemorial of Saintsbury and Lanier, bless me as I embark upon a metrical analysis . . .

Not quite. By value I mean I like it. No need to anatomize it for once. How even begin the notation? Without killing it, I mean. In this mood, I mean.

Instead a simpler point, kind of to the side. We know that music and songs are associated with sound, the art of sound and vice versa. One way we see Frank's devotion to how his prose *sounds* is – perhaps incidentally; I don't think so – in how *songs* and *singers* permeate his prose. It makes good common sense that a writer interested in how his prose sounds would be interested in singers and songs. Anyway, it makes sense.

Part of what songs do in Frank's fiction is to remind the reader that there is a relationship between art and the body. In the case of a song it reminds us that that's a voice coming out of a body. Frank reminds us all the time of how writing itself comes out of a body. A body often sick. He reminds us that's a voice that you hear. And also a performance, almost always a performance. So the songs are part of a continuum of art that comes out of a human body. As such, they can, like the body, be sick. They thereby also ground art in something very real. This is what the songs mean. Sometimes also ethnic pride. (Pride?) Actually those two things – the connection to the body and the real things of the body and the Italian connection – are interrelated not only in the song motif (such as it is) but all throughout the prose. And there's the connection of songs to art in general as a worthy pursuit. To put it mildly.

Note: It should of course be clarified that by "body" is also meant "mind."

To see some examples, deadly examples – his "character" Lucchesi says "there are no 'examples,'" of examples he is most contemptuous – we begin at *The Edge of Night*. We were talking about Frank's fictions and though *The Edge of Night* is no fiction *per se*, it is nonetheless an important hinge in the corpus (the body has too many doors: check the back door, blood on the toilet paper, stranger with sickle) and upon it hinges an anecdote about fiction, performance, the destiny of names.

It was strange and not necessarily easy for me to call Frank Frank, which he will understand, since like me he was raised right. You say Mister This and Missus That and Professor So-and-So. Then I suppose at a certain point you make some kind of transition. To us students back then, though, Frank was Professor Lentricchia but he was also, among the most compelled of us, Frank. But that was a kind of private language between a few people. But Frank, who if anybody ever did, deserved a wise guy nickname, was also briefly The Trick. It didn't stick but it wasn't a bad name.

And basically that was the class dialectic. The

tricks were being deployed but openly, frankly. The Frank Trick. The true tricks of the trade had to do with writing and reading. That was the stuff. We didn't actually come up with any ideas about the name at the time. That's me after the fact, thinking it over while reading Frank. You talk about a teacher. A lot of time it hinged on how a passage sounded, or a word, which always had a history and if it didn't have a reason for being there, was deemed a trespasser. *Note to self: difference b/w "sound" as aural sensation and "sound" as in just right (a loud sound versus a sound practice).*

The Edge of Night ends with Frank's father saying, "Frank, the fakery!" Part of the frank fakery in the memoir is Frank performing the role of the singer: "I croon out of the black part of my soul," he says in a revenge fantasia. "And then we would all sing the multicultural rag," he writes elsewhere. The book begins more or less with his mother, who "is prone to opera. She talks in arias." Sometimes too the son:

> Midnight. I take the poem. *The Waste Land* in one sweeping glance, one breath, performing it for my mind's ear, with fierce joy, like an extended aria marked *legato*, imagining myself a virtuoso tenor of criticism, in the *bel canto* style. I cannot fall asleep, and in the dark I luxuriate in my perform-ance, standing ovations, shouts of *Encore!*

But his "words are no good, the words about the magic do not communicate the magic," the "magic exceeds my words about the magic." Well, I don't know. That was pretty good. Maybe I'm just predisposed to like it. Maybe some gene. I wouldn't really know. I'm not really a scientist.

While we're at it, here's another passage appropriate to the moment that's got something about songs in it, something that sings to it:

I like the histories of words, their relatives, close, distant, and imaginary. I like Italian words, *sì certo!* For example: *elaborare*. I like the annotation of annotation. Noun, from the Latin *annotation: an*, to, and *notation*, a marking, from *notare*, to mark. I have a relative, uncle by marriage, named *Notaro* (Antonio), close reader, marker of texts. At twelve I watched him from across the room, he was so thick-wristed, marking a racing form, half listening to Puccini, shoeless and lounging, and Di Stefano (the tenor who ravishes me first) pouring it out. I associate the opera of nineteenth-century Italy with this raffish man named Notaro, vaguely criminal in manner, who does not read, or need, books. Intense textual concentration, pencil in a bone-crushing hand (he looked like Valentino), against a background of soaring lyric tenor. I started to associate myself with the opera of nineteenth-century Italy at twelve, watching him, so engrossed, escaped from me, in the room but not in the room. Large Italian-American reading: concentrating for his freedom, happy.

It is only a matter of time until the transformation is complete, the apotheosis reached: that is, the scene in *Lucchesi and The Whale* in which Thomas Lucchesi replaces Pavarotti in *La Bohème* at La Scala. However, if I may venture a personal opinion, my favorite musical moment in *Lucchesi and The Whale* is not the transformation of Lucchesi into a makeshift Pavarotti, central though that scene is to understanding Frank's idea about writing as performing and how closely that idea is shaped by an understanding of opera, opera as a model for what he means. Weak word there, "understanding" – a *something* of opera . . . To say nothing of the body, how uncomfortable it is. On the plane. In the seat. Backstage. How pained . . .

No, my favorite musical moment in *Lucchesi and The Whale* is when Thomas Lucchesi goes to meet Thomas (Three-Finger Brown) Lucchese, "who actually did violence." The gangster is "morosely watching the *Arthur Godfrey Show* and awaiting the appearance of Arthur's special guest, the stunning Phyllis McGuire, lead singer of The McGuire Sisters." Has a tumor, is in love with Phyllis. "Just before Phyllis came on, Giselle MacKenzie, the cute Canadian redhead, sang 'My Funny Valentine.' While she was singing the part about you're not good looking by any standard but I love you anyway, Three-

128

Finger looks at Tommy and Tommy doesn't look away. Finally, Phyllis, who glows. Three-Finger says to Phyllis, 'Sing "Sincerely" by yourself.' But Phyllis doesn't sing without her sisters."

At the Abbey now: "And I am hurtled into boredom by readings from the Bible not done with keen attention to the aesthetic values of rhythm and sound. Unless they come across as beautiful performances of great writing, poetry, not conversation, I cannot, and do not, listen."

Or in *The Music of the Inferno*, a picture of a just-born, about-to-be orphaned baby: "Mouth wide open, screaming and cavernous, like an opera singer in the climactic scene." Lots of things are like opera, "mountains like arias" (*The Edge of Night*), "arias of reason, arias of passion" (*Johnny Critelli*). The melodrama. The sound. Girl and boy stuff. Play acting, life and death. Lots of things are like the end of an opera, a terminal disease (redundant), like Utica: "It is an astonishment, but true, that nine histories of Utica have been written . . . This fact alone tells us that Utica is quite rare. Like a vicious and mysterious disease." Writing is a disease and a cure for the disease.

Of all the characters, Lucchesi especially is a case study for this medico-literary paradox. Ruth, whose heart murmur is real, except when she records it, may conclude about Lucchesi's health concerns what she concluded about his jealousy: "It's an act. Italian Opera." If so, the act is fundamental to the man. The man's doctor says, "I saw him at the clinic once for an imaginary illness, a Lucchesi specialty. He said, The dead weep for joy when their books are reprinted – that is my hope for death." The doctor says, "He tells me that his symptoms, whatever they might be, invariably disappear *on the way to see me*. This is a head case of a serious order." The same man who became Pavarotti, wetting his pants. The same who achieved tumescence while singing "Take Me Out to the Ball Game." This Mickey Mandolino of the nub does like to talk about baseball, as does the man who made him. To sing of it and other things. Today it is raining a little. It's a good day to think about Frank and write. And as I write, the Yankees are making their customary charge. The season has meaning. Crack of a bat on a ball. Cleats on dirt. The crowd erupts in peace.

Frank Lentricchia's Creative Quest

Traversing the Primal Fantasy
of the Modern Writer

DANIEL T. O'HARA

AND GINA MASUCCI-MACKENZIE

> The artist, like the God of the creation, remains within or behind or beyond or above his handiwork, invisible, refined out of existence, indifferent, paring his fingernails.
>
> James Joyce,
> *A Portrait of the Artist as a Young Man* (1915)

I

Although he has continued to write criticism, Frank Lentricchia in the last decade has primarily devoted himself to creating fiction, short novels often experimental in nature. These novels are filled with mordant irony and savage satire, and through the vehicles of comic surrogates, the satire and irony take on a self-reflexive cast. We believe that this critical self-judgment is no epiphenomenal feature of his fiction, but rather its basic substance. To put our argument in the proverbial nutshell, Lentricchia's fiction pursues the quest of exposing to severe critique the fundamental fantasy of the modern writer. This primal fantasy, given fullest expression in his fiction in "Chasing Melville" in *Lucchesi and The Whale*, is that of autopoesis, the romantic dream of radical self-creation, in which the given self is entirely re-made into the created aesthetic self, solely existing in the work of art one has produced as its hidden (or not so hidden) god, its defining principle of selection or style.

That the ordinary world of the traditional realistic novel or indeed of the common world of everyday life it attempts to represent would be imaginatively (or otherwise) transformed by the fulfillment of such an autopoetic fantasy is a consequence devoutly to be wished for by most modern writers. As Lentricchia and Jody McAuliffe have argued in *Crimes of Art and Terror*, such a fantasy puts them, willy-nilly, imaginatively in league with terrorists from the time of the French Revolution to that of today's so-called Islamic fascism. As our epigraph makes clear, the primal fantasy of the modern writer is usually expressed ironically, so that its romantic grandiosity is balanced by the critical aesthetic distance such irony affords, in the case of our epigraph, by Joyce's putting the fantasy of being sui generis in the mouth of Stephen Dedalus, who by this point in Joyce's ironic narrative has been repeatedly subject to the reader's critical scrutiny.

This division of the writer into given self (or its fictionalized representative) and godly aesthetic ideal appears in the great works of such romantic poets as Blake or Wordsworth as the conflict between everything in the self that would block creativity (the Specter or Selfhood in Blake and Wordsworth, respectively), and the creative imagination's apparently absolute freedom (most often just called the Self). Victorian and early modern writers present this division as one between the claims of commercial society and the radical temptations of aesthetic individualism. But sometimes, as in "The Jolly Corner" (1908) by Henry James, this division is played on ironically so that the protagonist, an expatriate aesthete on returning to America after thirty-three years to secure the financial future of his property, seeks to confront the ghost of his unrealized entrepreneurial promise by haunting the empty house of his childhood and summoning up and then bringing this ghost to bay.

As Harold Bloom in a series of studies famously develops the case about the primal fantasy of the modern or post-romantic writer, the conflict between culture and imagination takes on a clinical therapeutic form reminiscent of both Blake and Freud: the would-be visionary must confront and slough off the Specter or Super-Ego of self-conscious repression of literary predecessors if he or she is to achieve the fullest expression of authentic individual creative power, which in the final phases of a writer's career often means sloughing off or subjecting to self-critique this very self-consciousness as it would succumb to the apocalyptic autopoetic fantasy. In sum, the wound itself must become, dialectically, the source of the cure.

How this plays out can be usefully seen, we think, in terms of Lacanian psychoanalysis. The final stage of this therapy requires that the patient, without the support of the conventional symbolic order of society, face in progressively larger doses the primal imaginary fantasy veiling the fundamental trauma or psychotic gap in the psyche's structure – that psychic reality Lacan calls "the Real" – so that the psyche's linguistically based structure may be revised by being pieced together in a more creatively woven text, or if you prefer, in less destructive and self-destructive ways. Though therapy is Lacan's preferred form of such psychic transformation, in his seminar on Joyce Lacan describes how the modern writer, in this case Joyce, may transfigure his most potentially debilitating symptom into what he terms "le sinthome," that is, into the thread that re-weaves the psychic structure into a greater imaginative being. In Joyce's case, his symptom is the profound disconnection he experiences between the formal features of words, especially their sonorous rhapsody, which so delights him, and their meanings about which he ultimately cares little. The apocalyptic transformation of this symptom into *Finnegans Wake* constitutes, for Lacan, Joyce's "sinthome," the prosthetic device, as it were, that supplements by reweaving together the broken text of his otherwise psychotic structure of mind. Our argument here is that in his fiction Frank Lentricchia pursues such a creative quest by traversing the symptom of the ambiguous role of woman in the modern world, so that certain of his women characters become not only muse-figures for their artistic or would-be artistic male companions, but that they become for themselves genuinely self-transfiguring, as artists of their own lives. The imaginative world of his fiction projects what otherwise could be a symptom into Lentricchia's self-healing "sinthome."

II

The title character of *Lucchesi and The Whale* longs to engage in autopoesis, using Melville and his great novel as a template for his own self-creation. Without a female muse figure in close proximity, however, Lucchesi quickly moves from autopoetic to auto-pathetic. Lentricchia manipulates his own post-modern narrative structure to mock Lucchesi, who cannot create a grand, or even new story of himself, but instead is forced to write a manifesto on *Moby-Dick*. In the central, "Chasing Melville" section of the novel, the reader is faced with this manuscript.

To begin, Lucchesi must murder the father, in this case, Melville's classic, so as to rewrite it himself, through critical interpretation. To complete the assassination, Lucchesi denies the text its name, stating in a faux "Author's Note," "I, Lucchesi, assume that you have read, or more likely have heard bespoken, a certain portly tome of prose fiction, which I must not name. I assume that you know this tome, which you might falsely name, concerns a character who hunts down, in order to murder, a certain whale, which also must not be named, and which you confuse with the name of the yet-to-be-named tome."

As a writer, Lucchesi has fallen prey to Bloom's classic anxiety of influence. Lentricchia forces his character, a man uncertain about his own roots as an Italian American, to trace his literary lineage to one of the greatest American novels of all time. This subjects his protagonist to a multiplicity of difficulties, that he cannot face, and chooses to displace onto Melville, the original author, his own analysis of the text. Describing Ishmael, Melville, and himself, Lucchesi pontificates,

> A dead father. An emotionally remote mother. Double invisibility of the parental unit. What more liberating circumstances for the artist who can emerge only by rising over his pathetic humanity? And so he seizes his circumstances in diseased desire to be bereft of biological parents, to make himself mythic inhuman, thinking that, in the absence of evidence of divine genesis, he will think of himself as an orphan, because he thinks that the condition of the orphan is the precondition of an outrageous orphic . . . upon a presumed freedom to replace this unhappy world of his birth with self-born, self-delighting, self-affrighting words.

To replace the world with words sounds like reversal of some obscure Heideggerian notion, but is more immediately problematic for Lucchesi than high literary theory.

Lucchesi's quest relies on the consistent absence of the mother figure for his new self-birth. The mother-figure, representing a simultaneously nurturing and erotic force, that could actually enliven the drive, is missing, but Lucchesi does not recognize this as a problem until the very end of the novel, when he meets Ruth. Until that point, Lucchesi uses Melville's text, one necessarily void of female figures, one that replaces the feminine muse figure with the demonic natural world, as his starting point for self-generation. The text cannot be both mother and father, and his response to it, is not an original fiction, or sinthomatic creation, but a work of criticism, placed ironically in the center of the Symbolic order.

Only when Lucchesi finds Ruth the stewardess on an Alitalia flight appropriately back to his "fatherland" is Lucchesi able to abandon his textual anxiety and reach a new state of being. As he explains Wittgenstein's comments on naming, he proclaims, "My dear Ruth, the actual death of a man is incidental to his true life in culture and history. We achieve transcendence of the body." The transcendent moment, though, does not come through writing, as Lucchesi formerly believed it could, but through intercourse with his newly found muse. The body, not the text, or the name inscribed on it, has the power to encourage a new level of being. Lucchesi does not quite achieve that level in his novel, but with Ruth's help, in her tale, Lentricchia's follow-up *The Book of Ruth*, does find a new facet of living, with and through his muse.

When Lucchesi accompanies his far more talented and innovative photographer/wife to Baghdad, his work turns, not his usual postmodern nonsense, but to more traditional narrative roots based on the stories of Utica, his childhood home. Ruth, the muse figure, enables Lucchesi to create his true voice, which is ironically never fully heard, because of his subsequent kidnapping and probable murder.

Ruth is forced to return to her art so that she can be Lucchesi's muse. As a young woman, Ruth was an artist, photographing images of Cuba that gained fame for being totally apolitical in a pre-missile crisis climate. Faced with the murder of a child, she abandons her art, until it is her art that will enable her to fulfill her duty as muse. If she agrees to photograph Saddam Hussein in Baghdad, *The New Yorker* will publish and publicize Lucchesi's fiction. As muse figure she has no choice.

When Lucchesi is kidnapped and probably killed in Baghdad, Ruth returns to the states, to more fame, that she, for the second time in her life, eschews. She turns from photography to a new art, the art of self-creation. Instead of staying in their cabin, Ruth moves back to Utica, the place of Lucchesi's childhood, to fashion herself into Angie, a long-dead beautician. Lentricchia writes, of the current beautician, another Angie who tells Ruth the story of the former salon owner, ". . . because you [Ruth] remind me a lot of her." Ruth, when asked, replies that her own name is Angie after which she gains some weight, starts wearing unneeded glasses, ". . . house dresses and two pairs of what the fashionable call mules, but which on Mary St., according to Angie, are called a slide." This transformation of Ruth into Angie ends the novel, leaving the reader feeling a bit disconcerted, yet comfortable.

Lucchesi's death has taken Ruth's desire for the avant-garde. She knows that she must refashion herself, in light of his death, but chooses not to create something new, but to recreate a personage from Lucchesi's childhood, as a means to be closer to him. His death has left the muse-aspect of her character without a target. By making herself into an image from his past, she is able to reconnect with him.

The concept of connection and recreation of an image also dominates Lentricchia's newest novel, *The Italian Actress*. In the novel, Jack, a videographer, made stale by years of university teaching, begins a journey back to life and art when he resides with Claudia, based on (who is the actual actress), of *8½* fame. Throughout the novel, Jack is enamoured with, but unable to make love to Claudia, the object of his sexual desire since childhood. Only after Jack films his new, disturbingly scientific pornography, and then destroys it at her bequest, is he able to have sex with her. Their relationship cannot last though, as Claudia realizes that Jack is in love with her image, not her current physical being. She, twenty years older than he, considers herself " . . . in the last phase." He fights that image saying, "I don't want you to be at the end. Or in the final phase. I don't want any phases." As an artist, he has created an image, but as a muse, Claudia knows that image is not enough.

Instead of helping him to find his art, Claudia as muse, helps Jack the artist find his way through art to conventional life. Jack ends the novel teaching film, hosting dinners, and feeding his dog.

Lentricchia's characters reverse the traditional connotation of autopoesis. A reader expects a novel's artist figure to do novel things, but Lentricchia's characters, instead of making themselves into people on the exciting fringe of society, move from that fringe into conventional existence. Such ironizing of autopoetic possibility also leads to a reinvention of the muse figure. Lentricchia's perverse muses help their artists to the conventionality that is typically considered the death of art, leaving the reader to judge whether or not this is accurate.

In *Lucchesi and The Whale*, Melville's text acts as Lucchesi's muse. Tied to an insurmountable work of literature, Lucchesi is not propelled forward but stunted in his growth. The muse is the written word and the word, taken by him as fact, cannot be adequately explained, or altered; the tangibility of the muse figure causes its failure. Without sufficient room for growth, Lucchesi is stifled by his own muse.

In *The Book of Ruth*, the tangible word is replaced by the transitory image. Ruth is a photographer, able to grasp in an instant, a lifetime of words. While words, for Lucchesi, have the constancy of water, images, for Ruth have the combustible potential of fire. When working with them, she makes them come alive because of their latent fire. Lucchesi writes, stuck in a meaningless career; Ruth's career too is stagnant until she must move to capture the images. Literally, Ruth only truly lives in her text when she is in Baghdad. The muse of her image has forced her to change locales. As she physically breaks with her routine life, she is impelled to make brilliant art. She does not, however, make herself over in a lasting fashion. Once she returns to Utica, after Lucchesi's kidnapping, the images are gone, and she undoes herself, turning only into Angie, a figure who already existed. Ruth's muse must be in motion to be effective, and when Ruth stops moving, she can only choose a life already lived.

Carrying forth the concept of the intangibility of the image is the muse Claudia. Before Jack is able to consummate his relationship with her, the omnipresent image of her former self haunts him. Her impossible sexuality on film impels him to create his own version of sexuality on film, one notably devoid of the romantic notions he associates with her. Once he has finished filming with Sigismondo and Isotta, Jack returns to Claudia, able to have intercourse with her, but once the sexual component of their relationship is realized, Jack's work ceases. Contact with the muse removes her mystery and forces the artist away from the self-creation she once engendered.

III

This ironic conclusion testifies more to Jack's damaged psychology than it does to anything about the nature of the muse/creator relationship as it manifests itself for Lentricchia himself. For, what he, in fact, dramatizes in the fiction, reaching a provisional climax in *The Italian Actress*, is the muse-figure losing her constraining role as enabling strait-jacket for the crazed artist, and gaining the condition of possibility to become a creator in her own right, too. The muse as creator, the creator as muse, replaces the splitting of these psychic functions and their displacement onto separate figures or characters, so that the subjectivity of and in the Lentricchia fictional text is equally "male" and "female," if we still want to use such designations, even provisionally. As in James' late novels, the symptomatic relationship to women characters in the fiction has in fact become the sinthome of Lentricchia's self-renewing, self-transforming, self-delighting creativity, beyond the inherited script of the post-romantic situation of the modern artist. By traversing the primal fantasy of such art, as Slavoj Zizek might say, Lentricchia's fiction opens the prospects for a transformation of the writer's self-mythology, beyond gender or other prescribed limitations. This is transcendence, however, not dependent on apocalyptic violence and destruction. Like nature, the still sad music of humanity can be attended to, rather than used as an excuse for embracing any terrible beauty.

Frank Lentricchia

An Interview by Thomas DePietro

Thomas DePietro: Why is there a picture of Mickey Mantle at your Duke website?

Frank Lentricchia: I didn't want my picture put up on the website – I'd become unpredictably camera-shy and my boyhood idol had just died. The consequence of this little joke was that a person I hadn't seen in years emailed to say "Nice pic, Frank, you haven't much changed." Subsequent conversations convinced me of his sincerity. I felt at the time, and still feel, that I should correct his impression. But I didn't. And I won't.

TDP: What role do sports play in your life?

FL: Sports – specifically, and only, baseball and the Yankees – give me liberation from intellectual life. And nonintellectual life. I escape everything – for awhile. But when the Yankees lose, somebody has to pay. In the end, of course, it's me. I require the impossible: an undefeated season, from Opening Day to the last game of the World Series. My wife says that proves I'm the secret son of George Steinbrenner.

TDP: How do sports figure into your life as a writer and intellectual?

FL: Sports are important subjects between male writers and intellectuals, especially when they're pals. Sports talk is our secret weapon. Without it we'd find it even more difficult to bear one another's presence. Because we males are uncommonly sensitive. What do I know of general import concerning the subject of sports and male writers and intellectuals? Sports talk allows me to bear myself – I know that.

TDP: What's your family history?

FL: My grandparents – all four – were born in the South of Italy and came to this country along with millions of others from their region in the early 20th century, to escape poverty and a hopeless way of life. They had no education. None. My parents were not permitted schooling beyond the 8th grade – then it was off to work to support the family. When I was a child, my mother would say, so many times, that it was necessary not to repeat their lives – that I should go to high school. In her mind, high school was the enchanted goal. At some point, it dawned on them that even college might be possible. Graduate school left them speechless. When I was a child my mother punctuated all her advice about getting an education by showing me her rough, heavily calloused hands: she was an assembly line worker. My parents regarded my life as an actual miracle. More than once, my mother said, "We're not smart, how could we make you?" I told her that I didn't think of myself as smart – that I was just following her example – working hard. My professional life made my parents happy – to the extent that it even overcame their sadness for the various disasters of my private life.

TDP: What role does ethnic Utica play in your intellectual and writerly life?

FL: I grew up in a heavily Catholic Italian-American town. There were Italians, as we thought of ourselves, and then there were all the others whom we called "Americans." Not until I went off to college did I know any Americans. So the voices, the colors and rhythms of working class Italian-American people and culture shaped my sense of who I was. I felt myself on the inside of an ethnic enclave that was on the outside of American life. And that, I think, had something to do with my first career – in literary criticism and theory. Whatever was in academic dominance I looked at skeptically and even with hostility. I believe that I had good intellectual reasons for my stance, but there was something instinctual at work too.

TDP: Getting back to the role of photographs in your career – a major character in *The Book of Ruth* is a photographer – was it a conscious decision to have author photos on your most controversial books that show you looking tough? Are they the real source of your reputation as "the Dirty Harry of literary criticism?"

FL: My writing on literary theory was all about taking down what was fashionable at elite institutions – if it was fashionable it couldn't be right. And that got me the nickname in the *Village Voice* of the Dirty Harry of literary criticism – this lone gun approach. The tough-looking book jacket photo you refer to was another joke. I didn't feel comfortable among academics – still don't – and didn't want to look like one. Hence the photo against a graffiti-smeared wall featuring phone numbers that promised various unmentionable delights. Tough is such a joke. I was a book worm nerd in a neighborhood where one needed to hide one's nerdish nature. And I hid it pretty well; I survived. Maybe I'm still after all these years trying to pass, to hide it. I wonder what my students see when I stand before them? What do I want them to see? The Tony Soprano of literary criticism?

TDP: How does this figure into your fiction?

FL: As for my second career. My fiction is inhabited in my first 3 novels by Italian-American voices. Those books were set in my hometown. They have an autobiographical underpinning. Which is not to say that they are autobiography. Proust said it best: "I invented nothing; I imagined everything." My characters in those first fictions bear names of members of my family: But those family members do not exist as they are, or were – they're not all of them dead yet, though I approach that final loss when I can only say, I'm next. They exist in my fiction as they should be, as inhabitants of an imaginative world.

TDP: Is there an ethical issue here?

FL: No doubt. I've tried not to do anything but elevate my family characters as figures of vivid energy and life – enhancing force. But one uncle didn't think so and went to his grave totally alienated from me. I've never thought that creating a fictional world had much to do with making up names. In more recent novels some chief characters continue to bear Italian names, but they are not ethnic characters. They live in a wider world of art and politics. They've left the old neighborhood.

TDP: So why do you continue to give your characters Italian names?

FL: Because they ease the flow of imagination as some important drugs for older men ease the flow of urine. Real names are the Flomax of my mind. Writing for me is expression (a pressing out) of that which, if not expressed, will poison my psyche. After it's all let out, I feel better. Violence, for example, is done in my fiction – as in *The Knifemen* – so that I don't have to do it in what we call the real world.

TDP: Why do you think your theory work was so popular in the academy and beyond?

FL: My work on theory had a surprisingly (for theory books) wide readership because it said that literature and life itself were more complicated – I mean theory-resistant – and more humanly rich than theory, which I was at pains to show was in both idiom and method divorced from everything except conversation with other theorists. Philosophical discussion is by nature, of course, abstract – and needs to be – but the sort of abstraction that disfigures most theory is bloodless through and through, with no possibility of alighting on earth. Granted, by definition all *discussion* of literature flies above the *actual* terrain. Theory tends to fly at 45,000 feet, like bomb-laden B-52s. Literary criticism ought to be like a Piper Cub: low and slow and bomb free. Do Piper Cubs exist anymore? Does literary criticism?

TDP: How did it affect you when conservative critics started focusing on you as one of the prominent "tenured radicals"?

FL: Conservative critics of me as a tenured radical – they include Lynne Cheney – had to ignore the inconvenient fact that leading edge theorists abominate my work for its harsh treatment of their theories. They had to ignore the fact that I teach almost exclusively canonical Western writers of male gender. These so-called conservatives, who bitch about the politicization of the academy, are digesting sour grapes. They're whiners who want their own political agendas to have more academic play. So where are those people, anyway? Outside the academy making more money than the critics they whine about. Why don't they come in, take a big cut in pay, and change the landscape? And then there is this: by their complaints – if you read them carefully – you see they haven't read well the work they bitch about. They're largely wrong, objectively speaking, about what they see is in the work. Their description of my books about theory as "bibles of political correctness" is ignorant. Oh, I'll give them this – and it's no small thing: they're right about the trashing that great writers routinely undergo for supposedly violating oppressed minorities.

TDP: It seems like your big shift from litcrit was announced by your memoir, *The Edge of Night*. What was the impulse to write about your life as a father, husband, son, and academic?

FL: The memoir book, *The Edge of Night*, had a double origin. In the late 80s, I had a growing sense that academic literary criticism was no longer interested in the art of literature and its power to reveal the world in fresh ways. And then, in April of '91, I made a trip to a trappist monastery in South Carolina, where I spent 4 days living the life – praying the hours around the clock, rarely talking. What I saw embodied at Mepkin Abbey was an idea I derived from reading Thomas Merton years ago: that monks were the best examples of the sort of pure devotion that ought to define the life of a writer. I was enthralled. When I left, I was asked by one of the monks to "write about us" because "you're a writer." I'd never considered myself a writer in that sense, but felt that this man couldn't be refused. I wanted to believe that he knew something about me that I didn't. So I wrote a piece about my experience at Mepkin Abbey which *Harper's* took and I was off. The exhilaration of excavating my own inner world rather than someone else's was indescribable. That feeling, together with the sense that literary criticism, as an act of patient descriptive homage, was no longer respected, or even wanted, turned me in a new direction. A less noble motive is this: I'm easily bored. I needed to do something different – write in a different way – or suffer a kind of death. I chose to live. In one way, nothing has changed: as a literary critic I wrote about writers; as a fiction writer my central characters are almost all artists of one sort or another.

TDP: Academics aren't known for revealing personal secrets or confessing their mistakes in print.

FL: I don't believe that in *The Edge of Night* I revealed secrets in the sense that I was telling readers about actions that I performed that might have (or should have) been kept out of view. The book is mainly about imaginary relationships to real people and real places. Memoir as a kind of fiction – a fiction of autobiography. Not about what is, but about what is desired in my relations with, say, my father, or with W.B. Yeats, who, obviously, I never met, but whom I *do* meet in my desire-fueled memories. A life I never lived, but wanted to live with my kinsman, T.S. Eliot – a relative of mine as much as any blood relative I ever had.

TDP: Not long after the memoir came your essay saying goodbye to litcrit. What was it you were leaving behind?

FL: "Last Will and Testament of an Ex-Literary Critic" was a farewell to literary study dominated by political correctness, which really should be called political animus. I found it difficult and finally impossible to teach graduate students who were mainly interested in convicting canonical white male writers of crimes against humanity. I tried to stand against this in the classroom, but found it dispiriting to teach students who had no respect for literary values. The straw that broke the camel's back – I mean mine – was when on the first day we were to discuss a novel by Faulkner, and before I could get beyond the opening moment of my remarks, a student – white, male – declared that the first order of business was to stipulate that Faulkner was a racist. He actually said "stipulate." I replied that the immense formal challenges of the book would make it difficult for me to stipulate anything. No response. Then I urged him to maybe consider that all whites, including himself, maybe harbor a trace of racism in their hearts. No response. I wished I'd said that I'd prefer to roast in hell with Faulkner (if that's where he was) than to share space in heaven with him. Morally self-righteous literary academics are, many of them, at heart, book burners. Serious literature is their nightmare because it won't support simplistic moralism or programs for social change. Or programs of any kind. Serious literature is wayward.

TDP: Did your scholarly work on Don DeLillo have anything to do with your shift?

FL: It wasn't my critical writing on Don DeLillo's fiction that motivated my turn to fiction-writing. Many years before I'd been reading his work and I suspect now that experience was (and continues to be) an underground instigator. Not his subject matter, but the severe stylistic beauty of his writing captured me. And his irrepressible wit – the comic thrusts through even the darker corners of his imagination. He was, and is, a model of devotion to his art, just as the trappist monks are models of devotion. I'm moved by those who are devoted to a discipline. I'm not sure that I believe in God, but if God exists I'm certain that He expects us to be devoted to the gifts He blessed us with. I think it a sin not to be devoted, God or no God.

TDP: What are some of the other reasons for the switch to fiction?

FL: Many things had to do with the switch. My disenchantment with the academy; Father Leonard Cunningham at Mepkin Abbey; DeLillo's fiction; the feeling that I was finished as a literary critic; and a stint as an actor – the immediate cause, I'd say – because the assuming of roles is what we do when we make consciousness other than our own. And then there are all the subterranean causes I'll never know anything about. Those might be the most powerful ones. I've a suspicion that we can't know what makes us who we are and that trying to acquire such knowledge is not only pointless but damned unhealthy, the royal road to disconnection. Writers are self-preoccupied enough, don't you think?

TDP: That's for sure, though I've known a few who weren't. Let me ask you this: do you see an arc to the fiction, moving from familial history to the present?

FL: You think I can see the arc of my fiction? You may see it, I doubt that I can. The question assumes that a writer has privileged inside access to what his work is all about. If this were true, then the finest criticism of any writer would be produced by the writer himself. Not so. Writers are largely blind to their work's significance and meaning because so much of it comes from sources not rational, not critical. What comes from my unconscious is more easily seen by someone else.

TDP: So what do you see?

FL: For what it's worth, this: that from the beginning I've been preoccupied with the necessary selfishness of the artist – the solitude, the disconnection from others, the preoccupation with his internal life – even at the dinner table with loved ones and friends. And he knows this, and such self-knowledge produces, properly (says this Catholic boy) guilt – a sense of inhumanity even, because he chooses, knows he chooses, art over life. Push comes to shove: art over life. Yeats wrote that we must choose between perfection of the work and perfection of the life. I think I know something about the artist's choice. But the joke is on him. (Me.) He doesn't get perfection of the work, he knows this, and he's left with a life not nearly enough fully lived. His worst fear is that he hasn't lived at all. I've taken on that theme in everything I've written. Even in my books with a political subject – *The Music of the Inferno, The Book of Ruth* – my accompanying theme is psychological, the self-enclosing passions. Guilt in this matter is good. Very good. It brings one back to the dinner table – on occasion.

TDP: What's the role of women in these very male-centered narratives?

FL: I've always thought that the male-centeredness of my narratives has been overstated. The novel I've just completed, *The Italian Actress*, and the previous one, *The Book of Ruth*, are female-centered. Writers assume roles – I've been expanding my repertory. But think of Faulkner's repertory. What he does with animals. Not only in "The Bear" – in many of his novels, dogs especially have the weight of consciousness. That's what you call a repertory.

TDP: Here's the standard autobiographical question about your character Thomas Lucchesi, who appears in two of your novels. What's his relation to you?

FL: I can't do better on the connection between me and Lucchesi than R.M. Berry did in the *American Book Review*. "Lucchesi is Lentricchia's dour fantastic, an obscure novelist for whom nothing that comes naturally

158

comes naturally, hybrid of Orphic self-defeat and self-creation." I could never have said that because I never knew it. Writing is the unnatural act that comes naturally to me.

TDP: Meaning?

FL: I think it says that I'm a comfortable pervert.

TDP: What's your sense of the market for serious fiction?

FL: About the market for serious fiction I've nothing new to say. The marketing departments of the commercial houses – and many smaller ones – are in the saddle and ride mankind (to steal a line from Emerson). It's obvious that I'm incapable of writing commercially viable fiction, but if I ever did I'd cry – all the way to the bank.

TDP: How have your academic colleagues responded both to your attack on what they do and your turn to fiction?

FL: My colleagues didn't appreciate my attack on non-literary criticism posing as literary criticism. I heard the worlds "fouling the nest." On the other hand, for a period of almost three months I received letters of gratitude every day – no exaggeration – from teachers of literature from all around the country who were not working in elite institutions. They were at state colleges, obscure colleges, junior colleges, high schools. They wanted to tell me they supported my effort to restore literary study. They believed, as I did, that literature is a force in its own right, that literary study conducted as literary study could communicate unique values to the formation of a fully-equipped adult. I don't assume that my students wish to become literary critics or English teachers. I do assume that my students want to preserve their freedom in a culture that inundates them with messages – verbal and visual – whose purpose is to persuade them to ends subversive of their health – moral, mental, political, financial. I hope that close reading of literary messages – the method that I deploy in my classes – will help my students deal critically with all the media-propelled languages and images that flood and threaten to drown us daily. By "critically" I mean "independently." If we wish to preserve some measure of independence, we can't afford not to be close readers. In the classroom, I remain a literary critic.

TDP: And on the fiction?

FL: With the exception of two, my colleagues don't respond to my fiction. My suspicion is that most think I've lost my mind and feel embarrassed on my behalf. I want to be fair. Why should my colleagues be interested in my fiction when I'm not for the most part interested in what they do – except for two. For me, the most disenchanting thing about teaching in literary departments, for several decades, is that a bunch of people gathered together presumably because of common interests have no common interest. We don't talk about writing and creativity. If you want to talk about those things you need to talk to a writer.

TDP: Do you see any role remaining for criticism? The first Lucchesi novel could be seen as a type of literary comment, don't you think?

FL: *Lucchesi and The Whale* is all fiction – especially the long first person centerpiece – Lucchesi's monologue on *Moby-Dick*. Fiction in the form of an eccentric critical essay. The subjective world of my lead character as revealed through his encounter with a book that drives him to distraction.

TDP: Will you do any more criticism?

FL: I've taken up literary criticism again in modest ways. I'm doing a piece on the Joyce/Faulkner connection, another on E.A. Robinson, and yet another on the beginnings of modernist poetry in America. I'm doing this work to restore balance to my mental life. If I can, I'd like to letter in two sports.

TDP: Your forthcoming novel features a real person – Claudia Cardinale – as a major character. This isn't the first time you've used real people in your fiction. There have been cameos by Castro, JFK, and Saddam. Why put real people in a fictional world?

FL: Fiction is about the real world, so why not put real people in it? Castro, JFK, Saddam and don't forget O.J. Simpson, a sustaining figure in *The Knifemen*. And now Claudia Cardinale, the heroine and moral center of my forthcoming novel. How else to meet people I could never have met? They're all large public figures who exist for us as less than or more than human. Icons, images. What we can know about them, in the strict sense of knowing, tells us little, if anything, about their inner lives. They come to us in uncomplicated ways. The revolutionary, the tyrant, the tragic handsome prince, the Satan, the killer, the beautiful woman. They're not real. I need to imagine them in order to experience them as real – as real as myself with the colors of anxiety, self-doubt, depression, fragility, sadness. All the colors of mortality. Especially mortality. Famous real people allow me to enlarge my usual world. My responsibility is to make them less dismissible, complicated, sympathetic, more like you and me. Not to treat them with the mindless moral categories that drive our fundamentalist religious and political cultures.

TDP: What about family? You use them in *Johnny Critelli*. Do you have any special responsibility to them?

FL: How else live intimately with them except by imagining them? Especially now when so many are dead? We're circling back to the guilt of a writer who can't find time enough for intimacy in his non-writing life and tries to supplement that terrible lack, by how? By writing. We do what we can and hope we're not worthy of Ibsen's words in *When We Dead Awaken*: "The child of the mind first, the child of the body second."

Biographical Note

In 1986, Frank Lentricchia told an interviewer, "I'm not a gentleman scholar." This was not posturing: Lentricchia was born to working-class parents in Utica, New York, on May 23rd in 1940. Frank John and Ann Iacovella Lentricchia, children of immigrants from Southern Italy, both left school after the eighth grade to begin work. Young Frank attended the local public schools. His earliest enthusiasms were reading and baseball. He was graduated from Utica College in 1962, where his love of literature was further stimulated by inspiring professors, who encouraged him to attend graduate school. He earned his M.A. from Duke University in 1963, and his Ph.D. in 1966. At Duke he came under the influence of Bernard Duffey, a scholar of modern poetry, which would become Lentricchia's main area of interest as well.

In 1967, Lentricchia married Karen Young, with whom he had two daughters, Rachel and Amy. He also began his teaching career at UCLA, soon followed by a stint at UC, Irvine, where he was eventually promoted to full professor. His first two books were about modern poetry, and he then began to write more about literary theory, publishing his ground-breaking books in the early 1980s. His first marriage ended in divorce and, in 1973, he married Melissa Christensen, with whom he edited a book on Robert Frost. After a teaching post at Rice University, Lentricchia returned to his graduate school alma mater in 1984 as a Professor of English, and was instrumental in recruiting an all-star faculty to the school, turning this department of traditional literary studies into a hotbed of literary theory and criticism. Lentricchia's left-wing politics caught the attention of a number of journalists and neo-conservative polemicists, who sought to document the rise of campus radicalism at the time.

Throughout this period, Lentricchia was invited to lecture at major universities across the country, and served as the editor of two book series, one for The University of Chicago Press (*The Wellek Library Lectures*), and one for the University of Wisconsin Press (*The Wisconsin Project on American Writing*). He was also editor of *The South Atlantic Quarterly* from 1984 through 1991, when he became a chaired professor at Duke. During these years, his second marriage failed, and he began to drift from his previous work in theory. In 1994, after spending time at other non-academic pursuits, Lentricchia married Jody McAuliffe, a drama professor at Duke who also directs and writes. They have a daughter, Maeve, who was born in 1994. Lentricchia's first non-scholarly book, *The Edge of Night*, was published in 1994, and he soon followed with his much-noted essay in *Lingua Franca*, "Last Will and Testament of an Ex-Literary Critic," his farewell to certain types of academic criticism and theory. Though he did not completely abandon literary comment, Lentricchia from then on devoted himself to fiction. He continues to write and teach in Durham, North Carolina.

Selected Bibliography

Memoir

The Edge of Night (Random House, 1994).

Fiction

Johnny Critelli and *The Knifemen* (Scribner, 1996).
The Music of the Inferno (SUNY Press, 1999).
Lucchesi and The Whale (Duke University Press, 2001).
The Book of Ruth (Ravenna Press, 2005).
The Italian Actress (SUNY/Albany Press, forthcoming).

Nonfiction Books

The Gaiety of Language: An Essay on the Radical Poetics of W.B. Yeats and Wallace Stevens (University of California Press, 1968).
Robert Frost: Modern Poetics and the Landscapes of Self (Duke University Press, 1975).
After the New Criticism (University of Chicago Press, 1980).
Criticism and Social Change (University of Chicago Press, 1983).
Ariel and the Police: Michel Foucault, William James, Wallace Stevens (University of Wisconsin Press, 1988).
Modernist Quartet (Cambridge University Press, 1994).
Crimes of Art and Terror, with Jody McAuliffe (University of Chicago Press, 2003).

Edited

Robert Frost: A Bibliography, 1913-1974, with Melissa Lentricchia (Scarecrow Press, 1976).
Critical Terms for Literary Study, with Thomas McLaughlin (University of Chicago Press, 1990).
Introducing Don DeLillo (Duke University Press, 1991).
New Essays on White Noise (Cambridge University Press, 1991).
Close Reading: The Reader, with Andrew DuBois (Duke University Press, 2003).
Dissent from the Homeland: Essays after 9/11, with Stanley Hauerwas (Duke University Press, 2003).

Articles, Essays, and Reviews

The Yale Review, Journal of Aesthetics and Art Criticism, Salmagundi, Italian-Americana, Raritan, TriQuarterly, Critical Inquiry, South Atlantic Quarterly, American Literary History, Lingua Franca, London Review of Books, Harper's, Poetry and many other books and magazines.

Secondary Material

Reviews of the memoir and fiction

The Edge of Night

Daniel O'Hara. *boundary 2*, vol. 19, no. 1 (Spring, 1992), pp. 230-254.

Kirkus Reviews, Nov. 15, 1993, vol. 61, p. 1444.

Alice Joyce. *Booklist*, Dec. 15, 1993, vol. 90, no. 8, p. 734.

Nancy Shires. *Library Journal*, Jan. 1994, vol. 119, no. 1, p. 117.

Publishers Weekly, Jan. 10, 1994, vol. 241, no. 2, p. 51.

John Sutherland. *The New York Times Book Review*, Feb. 6, 1994, vol. 99, p. 24.

The New Yorker, April 25, 1994, vol. 70, no. 10, p. 111.

Paul Wilkes. *America*, May 7, 1994, vol. 170, no. 16, p. 18.

Noel King. *Australian Book Review*, Dec. 1994, p. 64.

Michael Gorra. *Transition*, no. 68 (1995), pp. 143-153.

Andrijka Kwasny. *Minnesota Review*, Spring 1998, no. 48/49, p. 227.

Kit Wallingford. *American Quarterly*, vol. 49, no. 2 (June, 1997), pp. 423-428.

Johnny Critelli and *The Knifemen*

Kirkus Reviews, Oct. 15, 1996, vol. 64, p. 1487.

Publishers Weekly, Nov. 4, 1996, vol. 243, no. 45, p. 64.

Lawrence Rungren. *Library Journal*, Nov. 15, 1996, vol. 121, no. 19, p. 91.

Vince Passaro. *The New York Observer*, Dec. 6, 1996, p. 27.

Lorna Sage. *The New York Times Book Review*, Dec. 29, 1996, p. 7.

L.S. Klepp. *Entertainment Weekly*, Feb. 14, 1997, no. 366, p. 56.

Irving Malin. *The Review of Contemporary Fiction*, Summer 1997, vol. 17, no. 2, p. 294.

Teri Reynolds. *The American Book Review*, Sept. 1997, vol. 18, no. 6, p. 20.

The Music of the Inferno

John Paul Russo. *Italica*, vol. 77, no. 3, (Autumn, 2000) pp. 440-441.
D. Quentin Miller. *The Review of Contemporary Fiction*, Fall 2000, vol. 20, no. 3, p. 153.

Lucchesi and The Whale

Jim Dwyer. *Library Journal*, Dec. 2000, vol. 125, no. 20, p. 189.
Publishers Weekly, Dec. 11, 2000, vol. 147, no. 50, p. 62.
Kirkus Reviews, Dec. 15, 2000, vol. 68, p. 1710.
R.M. Berry. *The American Book Review*, July 2001, vol. 22, no. 5, p. 1.
Thomas B. Hove. *Melville Society Extracts*, Feb, 2002, no. 122, pp. 29-31.
T.J. Gerlach. *The Review of Contemporary Fiction*, Spring 2002, vol. 22, no. 1, p. 139.
Jeremy Harding. *The London Review of Books*, Oct. 31, 2002, vol. 24, no. 21, p. 6.

The Book of Ruth

Kirkus Reviews, Sept. 15, 2005, vol. 73, no. 18, p. 996.
Thomas DePietro. *The American Book Review*, July-August, 2006, vol. 27, no. 5, p. 1.

There are numerous books, articles, and interviews concerning Lentricchia's career in criticism and theory. See Tim Dayton's article in *Twentieth-Century American Cultural Theorists*, ed. Paul Hansom, DLB, Vol. 246 (Gale, 2001) pp. 253-262.

Contributors

Nicholas Birns teaches at Eugene Lang College, The New School in New York City, where his specialities include Victorian and modern fiction and literary theory. His latest book, *Theory after Theory: An Intellectual History of Literary Theory from 1950 to the 21st Century*, was published in 2010 (Broadview Press). He co-edited *A Companion to Australian Literature since 1900* (Camden House, 2007), with Rebecca McNeer. His *Understanding Anthony Powell* (University of South Carolina Press) appeared in 2004. He has contributed to many periodicals including *The New York Times Book Review*, *Midstream*, *Arizona Quarterly*, *The Hollins Critic*, and *Studies in Romanticism*. He edits *Antipodes: A North American Journal of Australian Literature* and has been a visiting fellow in Sweden and Australia.

Andrew DuBois is Assistant Professor of English at the University of Toronto Scarborough. He is the author of *Ashbery's Forms of Attention* (University of Alabama Press, 2006) and is co-editor with Frank Lentricchia of *Close Reading: The Reader* (Duke University Press, 2003). He has also published essays, poems, and reviews in such journals as *American Literary History, Harvard Review, South Atlantic Quarterly,* and *The University of Toronto Quarterly*. Andrew was recently wed to poet Souvankham Thammavongsa and is invigorated in love.

Fred L. Gardaphe is Distinguished Professor of English and Italian American Studies at Queens College/CUNY. He is Associate Editor of *Fra Noi*, an Italian American monthly newspaper, editor of the Series in Italian American Studies at State University of New York Press, and co-founding-co-editor of *VIA: Voices in Italian Americana*. His books include: *Italian Signs, American Streets: The Evolution of Italian American Narrative* (Duke University Press, 1996); *Dagoes Read: Tradition and the Italian/American Writer* (Guernica, 1996); *Moustache Pete is Dead!: Italian/American Oral Tradition Preserved in Print* (Bordighera, 1997); *Leaving Little Italy: Essaying Italian American Studies* (SUNY Press, 2004); and *From Wiseguys to Wise Men: Masculinities and the Italian American Gangster* (Routledge, 2006).

Thomas Hove teaches in the Department of Speech Communication at the University of Georgia. He holds a Ph.D. in English from the University of Illinois at Urbana-Champaign and a Ph.D. in Mass Communications from the University of Wisconsin, Madison. He has published articles and reviews on Herman Melville, postmodern fiction, literary criticism, communication theory, and media studies. His current research explores the mass media theories of Jurgen Habermas and Pierre Bourdieu.

Gina Masucci-MacKenzie is an Assistant Professor at the Community College of Philadelphia. Her first book, *The Theatre of the Real: Yeats, Beckett, and Sondheim* was published in the Fall of 2008 by Ohio State University Press. Her essays have appeared in *The Journal of Modern Literature, The Annals of Scholarship*, and *The Ginko Tree Review*. She has co-authored several articles with Daniel T. O'Hara, and together they wrote the Introduction to the Barnes and Noble Classics Edition of Sigmund Freud's *The Interpretation of Dreams*.

Jody McAuliffe, a member of the Society of Stage Directors and Choreographers, was graduated from the Yale School of Drama, and teaches at Duke University. She has developed and directed new plays nationally and has recently published the novel, *My Lovely Suicides* (Ravenna, 2008). Her short fiction has appeared in *Southwest Review, Literary Imagination,* and *South Atlantic Quarterly*. She co-wrote (with Frank Lentricchia) *Crimes of Art and Terror* (Chicago, 2003), and edited *Plays, Movies, and Critics* (Duke University Press, 1993). She has edited a special issue of *South Atlantic Quarterly* on modern drama and is a contributor to *Vagant* (Oslo) and the *Journal of Modern Literature;* she also reviews theater for *Norwegian Shakespeare and Theatre Magazine*.

Daniel O'Hara is Professor of English and first Mellon Term Professor of Humanities at Temple University. He is the author of six books in criticism and theory, including *Empire Burlesque: The Fate of Critical Culture in Global America* (Duke, 2003); and co-editor of five collections of critical essays on modern theory and literature. His *Visions of Global America and the Future of Critical Reading* was published by the Ohio State University Press in 2009. Currently on study leave, he is completing two other books, *Experiments in Critical Reading: Nietzsche's Passion*, and a volume of poetry, *The Quantum Loves*.

Vince Passaro, a contributing editor of *Harper's*, works for the Yaddo Foundation. His novel, *Violence, Nudity, Adult Content* was published in 2002 by Simon & Schuster. His writing has appeared in *The New York Times Magazine, GQ, Open City, Elle,* and *New York* among others.

Philip Tinari is an art critic and curator based in Beijing and specializing in Chinese contemporary art. He is a frequent contributor to *Artforum* and has written for publications including *The New York Times Magazine, McSweeney's, Parkett,* and *The Wall Street Journal.*

171

He has written for and translated catalogues of Chinese art museums around the world. He advises Art Basel and Sotheby's on artistic developments in China, and directs the editorial studio and publishing house for Office for Discourse Engineering. He earned a B.A. in Literature at Duke, an M.A. in East Asian studies from Harvard, and was a Fulbright fellow at Peking University.

Kit Wallingford is a semi-retired Episcopal priest serving at Palmer Memorial Episcopal Church in Houston, Texas. Her vocational passion is contemplative spirituality, and she now reads Lentricchia's retreats at Mepkin Abbey very differently than when she wrote her review. She and her husband have two grown children and four grandchildren. Before her call to ordained ministry, she studied and worked in law for eleven years and then studied and taught English at Rice University. She has published the book, *Robert Lowell's Language of the Self* (University of North Carolina Press, 1988).

Jennifer Wellman is a Ph.D. candidate in English at the University of Maryland, College Park. She received her M.A. in English from the University of Maryland in 2006. Her interests include twentieth-century literature, British modernism, and self-reflexive fiction.